SYMBOLS
COME ALIVE
IN THE
SAND

This book is dedicated to my grandson, Noah,
who helps me keep on my path. He helps me stay in
touch with my own *inner* child and at
the same time know and relate to a very conscious,
earthy and beloved *outer* child.

SYMBOLS COME ALIVE IN THE SAND

Evalyn Dundas

COVENTURE

COVENTURE Coventure, Ltd. London, Boston
25 New Chardon Street #8748
Boston, Massachusetts 02114

Library of Congress Cataloging-in Publication Data
Dundas, Evalyn.
  Symbols come alive in the sand.
  Bibliography: p.
  1. Sandplay—Therapeutic use.   2. Psychotherapy.
3. Psychotherapy patients—Language.   4. Psycho-
therapist and patient.   I. Title.
RC489.S25D86 1990   616.89'1653   88-16211
ISBN: 0-904575-41-1

Printed in Korea

TABLE OF CONTENTS

PREFACE

Additional Impressions After the First Publication of

Symbols Come Alive In The Sand

It is now ten years since I first wrote anything about sandplay for publication. At that time nothing was in print in English about this technique of working with children or adults. I tried very dilligently to verbalize my thoughts and feelings about creative non-verbal healing, but found it almost impossible to write about in a meaningful and clear way; so I limited my writing to children's work only, even though I knew the adult process was just as healing with each person following his or her own individual journey, just as the child created his own scenario in depth. Recently, more and more has been written about sandplay, and it has become a popular medium with many therapists. I can hope only that all of us who dare to look so deeply into the psyches of individuals will remember that William Blake said long ago: "To see a world in a grain of sand," showing his deep affirmation of the holiness of life. This kind of seeing of images has never ceased for me, and has still that unique power of communication between myself as therapist and the creator of the scene. It seems still to allow the participant to experience his or her own true self. One young woman expressed it as a power and aid in sorting out her own personal journey and helping create her own myth. Another person said it allowed her unconscious to direct the conscious action and enabled her to create scenes and images of her own true self.

Yes, I do continue to use sandplay in my work, as well as dreams and active imagination and deep breathing, attempting always to resist advice giving and stating solutions or cures. To continually work on centering my "self" and to know the powerlessness of us all seems most important. I dare even to be a friend who cares. Recently, a dying woman taught me what true loving really is, and showed me, and I her, some of the power of healing as found in the symbols she produced in her sandplays. She and other adults and children continue to teach me a new love of self. Yes, once again my shelves are fuller of minatures than they were twenty years ago, and hopefully my understanding is deeper, as I continue to work enthusiastically with each person who teaches me as well, as I try to become more conscious each day. At present I spend much of my time teaching younger interns about sandplay and helping them experience more keenly their own creations.

With pleasure I add this one chapter on one woman's inner work and show some of her ritualistic creations she produced in the earth sand. She still is a young woman, and now a professional and mother and continues learning to truly live her life. For awhile she may have tried to climb the wrong ladder—don't we all?—but deep underneath she found her authentic self and allowed it to help program herself. I thank Mary for allowing me to write about her journey. It strengthens once more my belief that age can never limit our futures, unless of course we become victim of the process.

Evalyn T. Dundas

ACKNOWLEDGEMENTS

I wish to thank and acknowledge the two people who introduced me to sandplay as a therapeutic tool. The first is Harold Stone, a Jungian analyst practicing in Los Angeles. I met Dr. Stone in 1964 at a seminar given on new methods for treating schizophrenic children. I was invited to participate in this seminar because of my work with retarded children and with adults. At this seminar, Dr. Stone showed slides of sand pictures which had been made by schizophrenic and retarded children. He also discussed the therapeutic effects on children who had worked in the sand tray.

I was impressed by the earnestness of Dr. Stone, by his honesty, and by his friendliness and concern for his patients. I felt very strongly that sandplay therapy, as he presented it, was what I needed in my own work and was the tool I had been searching for. Dr. Stone invited me to observe his work and gave me the sources of written materials available at that time. I have thanked him before, but wish to do so again, for the encouragement and insight which he has generously shared.

I am also grateful to Dora M. Kalff, a Jungian analyst whose home is Zolliken, near Zürich, Switzerland. She is the author of the term "sandplay." Mrs. Klaff adopted the concept of sandplay from her work with Margaret Lowenfeld of the London Institute of Child Psychology.

I first met Mrs. Kalff in San Francisco where she was lecturing and holding seminars on sandplay therapy. I had further contact with her when I took three semesters of work at the C.G. Jung Institute in Zürich. I also studied with Mrs Kalff in her home at that time. One certainly feels, working with Mrs. Kalff, that she is the source of much deep warmth and instinctual understanding, or, in Jungian terms, that she embodies the essence of the Great Mother. Once I told Mrs. Kalff that I had this impression of her, and I asked her if it was difficult to keep from becoming inflated by the admiration of her students. She just laughed her deep and wonderful laugh, and it was clear that she was much too earthy for "flying off."

My most humble thanks go to this woman who has taught me so much. Most importantly, she helped me to know how to keep in touch with my own inner love and warmth, or with my own inner Mother. By continuing to be both an observer and a participant in this inner process of healing, coming from working with people in the sand tray, one's own psyche is touched and renewed as well.

Three other people are most important in making this book possible. Geneva Gates, though blind, sees deeply and so was able to reflect upon areas that were confused and unclear in the book. Susan Renfrew, the illustrator, made the drawings come alive. Words can not express my deep feeling for Susana McCall, my first editor. Her sense of honoring the other's creativity can come only from a deeply connected and loving soul.

INTRODUCTION

Sandplay is a unique therapeutic method. By playing creatively with a specially built sandtray, a person in therapy makes three-dimensional sand pictures. These give him a chance to express aspects of his imagination and deeply felt individual symbols that might otherwise never be communicated. He also comes into touch with thinking in images or symbols. By sharing this experience with a trained therapist, someone he can trust, a better understanding of his own feelings and life's patterns occurs, and healing begins to take place.

A trained therapist can learn to understand the deeper meanings of these expressions, thereby gaining fuller insight into what is happening to the client. However, an important part of any training period for a therapist planning to use the sandtray is to make a number of sand pictures himself. Although I had had many years of formal clinical training and experience before I started working with sand, I did not fully realize the value of sandtray therapy until I worked with sandplay myself. One must meet one's "own gods face to face," experiencing the fun of playing for its own sake and personally feeling how the sand works on the individual psyche. It is absolutely essential for the therapist himself to feel and know the anger, the joy and pain released through sandplay. When working with the sand, the therapist must take some emotional risks. If he is unwilling to do this at the outset, he will not be able to handle the highly emotional content of sandtray therapy when he works with his clients.

I have written this informal book to share the experiences of some of the children who used the sandtray for many types of problems. In this book, the children really tell their own stories. During the course of therapy, they shared with me the mysteries of their psyches and the miracles of their growth. It was a real privilege for me, and I would like to say how grateful I am to them for giving me this gift. I hope I can do justice to the mystery and magic that these children and I experienced in therapy.

I

SANDTRAY THERAPY

My first knowledge of sandplay came from two Jungian analysts: Dr. Harold Stone of Los Angeles and Mrs. Dora M. Kalff of Zollikon, Switzerland. Sandplay originated in 1928 with Margaret Lowenfeld at the London Institute of Child Psychology. Charlotte Buhler of the United States later made a kit available to clinicians, but it was Mrs. Kalff who made the term *sandplay* well known through her extensive travels and lectures, her book, *Sandplay, A Psychotherapeutic Approach to the Psyche*, and more recently her film on sandplay.

My work with sandtray therapy began when young teenagers who had been diagnosed as having minimal brain dysfunction and related emotional problems came to see me. Many had acquired rather thick and seemingly hopeless psychiatric files, and I felt any further diagnoses and interpretations were either inappropriate or unnecessary. Instead, I introduced them to this different form of therapy—working with the sandtray.

It is difficult to describe the joy and relief that came over the face of each child who entered my playroom. They came to the back yard by way of a long, narrow path. Most lingered outside for a few minutes to glance at the garden and the water wheel, but soon seemed ready to come inside and see what awaited them. After stepping into a fairly large waiting room, they finally entered the warm, smaller room where the sandtrays were. When they saw these, as well as the paint materials and a clay jar instead of a forbidding desk and chair, they were happy but also puzzled and curious.

The older teenagers would casually sit down, probably determined not to be trapped by all this. I found that if I did not say too much, the unexpected would always happen: sooner or later the sandtray wove its own magic. Once in a while, an older child simply wanted to talk, and that was all right, too.

DESCRIPTION OF SANDTRAYS

The sandtrays I use are the same dimensions — $19\frac{1}{2}'' \times 28\frac{1}{2}'' \times 3''$ — as those Dora Kalff recommends in her book. This size is quite important, as the sand tray should be within a person's visual and physical reach. For very young children, I set the sandtray on a lower table or place a sturdy foot-ladder in front of the regular table. This way they can climb up and down to choose the miniatures they need.

I keep two sandtrays ready at all time: one that can be dampened or flooded, the other kept dry. Because children often told me how good it felt to sift and play with the sand itself, I began to realize the importance of the sand's quality and texture. At first I bought commercial white sand that felt harsh and grainy. Later, I found softer and more malleable sand on certain beaches. It was then that I started collecting and sifting my own sand.

The color the sandtrays are painted can also be significant. Thus far I have painted mine blue or blue-green to represent water or sky. Other therapists choose to leave the wood in its natural state.

PLAYING WITH THE SANDTRAY

After the child has chosen which sandtray — the wet or the dry — he wants to work with, he then molds or plays with the sand for a while. This phase of therapy is important: both children and adults say it simply feels good to shape the sand. This begins the process of getting in touch with joyful — and painful — parts of themselves, until now hidden and unknown.

Playing in the sand is fun and creative. While most children usually know how to play, some who have had traumatic early childhood experiences feel constrained and are unable to do so spontaneously. Some even think it sinful to find fun in work. I have seen children who are deeply afraid to play. Somehow, many of us have forgotten the transforming and healing nature of creative play.

Once the child has molded the sand, he picks out the miniatures that strike his fancy. These miniatures, arranged on shelves that line three walls of my sand room, represent all facets of life, especially those of a child's life. Made of plastic, wood, metal or clay, they include trees, flowers and animals—fish, cows, horses, turtles, owls, dragons. And people from all walks of life stand on the shelves— soldiers, babies, females, males, Indians, cowboys, and so on. There are numerous religious figures, such as Virgin Maries, creche figurines, crosses, wise men, and Buddhas. And, of course, the miscellaneous miniatures like castles, bridges, stones, shells; pieces of wood and driftwood and glass abound. I have collected figures that play into a child's imagination—that is, whatever he can use to express a feeling, an emotion, or a situation.

There is no pattern or "right approach" to this process: a child may make intricate designs in the sand or simply place miniatures on a flat surface. Some talk while they play, weaving fabulous tales of fantasy and life experiences. Others remain silent, concentrating on their evolving picture.

When the sand picture is completed, I photograph it. When I do this, a child realizes his creation will live in a photograph. Later the slides help me to see shapes and forms that were not apparent when I first looked at the sand picture. Viewing slides alone, I gain a different perspective and fresh approach that add to my understanding.

UNDERSTANDING THE PROCESS

During the process, I always try to be sensitive to how the child is feeling. Often I can tell a great deal by observing carefully whether he chooses the wet box or the dry one, whether he starts shaping the sand or selecting the miniatures right away, or both simultaneously. I watch how he chooses his miniatures, what figures he selects and whether he later changes his mind and puts some back on the shelves.

When I am puzzled about why a child uses a particular miniature—a tree, a stone, a bridge, each a symbol for many things—I simply ask. The answer may be: "You know, trees are growing." Or, "Trees belong in the forest." Or, "A tree is a secret place." The answers are clues to the child's feelings and to *his* meaning of the symbol. For example, a stone or a rock can protect a favorite animal or represent the self. In each case, the child seems to know that whatever he chooses is special.

THE APPEARANCE OF UNIVERSAL SYMBOLS

Sometimes children use the miniatures to tell their own life history in a constructive and more conscious way. Yet enough is expressed by those who do not (if I listen inwardly as well as on the surface) for me to realize that they also attach common meanings to the same or similar miniatures. For both very open and very closed children, the sandtray allows deeper symbolic messages to become quite clear.

This is what makes sandtray therapy so vital: it builds understanding between therapist and individual. With the aid of the sandtray, I was able to communicate with these children in a different way. Not always sure of the meaning of certain symbols myself, I did not talk to them about the meaning of their miniature selections. Even when little is said about the sand picture itself, much is felt and understood about the scene's relevance to life problems and situations, and both therapist and client seem to intuit the meaning without words.

The recurring appearance of symbols in the sand pictures of each individual is one interesting aspect of sand therapy that is difficult to explain. These symbols are remarkable for their beauty and clarity. If the therapist is conscious of the various meanings of symbols, he can better relate them to the individual, and thereby aid and perhaps speed the healing process. He must know that the miniatures may represent images of the individual's deep psyche, and not just the immediate expression of a conscious thought. In other words, sandtray makers seem to be drawing upon a universal vocabulary of symbols.

This universal vocabulary can be amplified by more understanding of fairy tales and myths. We possess many myths and stories thousands of years old that still have a living, contemporary significance. Undoubtedly, these myths express some universal truths about the human condition, using symbols which have universal significance. Somehow, many children and adults have a natural understanding of myths and symbols.

The children who work in the sandtray come in direct contact with some of these universal symbols, and have a chance of understanding their lives in terms of them. Regardless of whether the individual understands the significance of the symbols, by using the sandtray he seems to feel liberated—as the more painful, angry and confusing parts of himself surface-and at last in touch what had been locked inside. Symbolically, a bridge is laid between fantasy and reality. In fact, a bridge is one of the most frequently used sand-tray miniatures once a person starts reaching out to life. As a transition and communications tool, the bridge is often a connection to life itself.

If the child can understand himself at this much deeper level, his life experience will be richer. By relating to active symbols and having a chance to live his own myth, a child can become truly alive in his own world.

Equally important, playing in the sandtray connects people at a very deep level. It helps them communicate their own feelings. Their own deepest symbols and myths, including those which have been dark and frightening, are brought to the conscious level by the means of the communication provided by the sandtray.

The sand brings out the creative side of the person who works with it. I have found this to be true with each of my clients. Through their own creative process, they find the road opens to lead them out of their difficulties.

Whatever place the individual reaches through sandplay therapy, one fact remains: somehow the psyche is touched and healing takes place.

2

STAGES OF DEVELOPMENT

Although the path of each person is different, three definite stages of development mark the way for each individual. Mrs. Kalff calls these three stages (1) the animal, vegetative phase; (2) the fighting phase; and (3) the phase of adaptation to the collective. Her stages seem to express accurately the process of growth involved in sandplay.

From my own experience, I find that the first few pictures communicate where a child presently is in life or where he is capable of being. These pictures can be very complicated, as if exposing all facets of the psyche. (For precisely this reason, the therapist *must* provide a safe environment and must honor the child's person). On the other hand, the first scenes may appear dry and lifeless, indicating a place of stasis. (Stasis is a medical term meaning retarded movement. Although it can occur in any stage, I feel it especially fits the first stage, the animal or vegetative phase). I always pay particular attention to the miniatures children use and to any clues they give me as to the symbolic meaning they attach to the pictures.

It must be noted, too, that a child who has been cut off from his natural mother at the time he is normally separating from his parents (one to three years) will try over and over to rebuild or reintegrate his wholeness by creating certain symbols, such as the circle, in the sandtray.

Then the boys enter the fighting or struggle phase, initially precipitated by some form of destruction. This may be a flood, a fire, a volcano erupting or a deadly war scene in which all old forms of life are destroyed. A few boys I have worked with do not set up battle scenes. One boy worked through his entire process by making complicated scenes of houses, sometimes in precarious positions, or on top of a high mountain in very simple but symbolic settings.

The girls I have worked with rarely destroy their scenes. Rather, they often wet and pound the sand, or paint what they consider ugly scenes. Occasionally they will pen up many animals they strongly identify with. They seem to use these miniatures to get in touch with the instinctual side of their natures. For girls, the general need seems to be to move inwardly rather than to go outside to start conflicts. In other words, the girls move into the second, or struggle stage, by containing and then freeing themselves from their instinctual identity. They may also act out fantasy scenes of places where people are evil, or of strange people on journeys.

When the boys reach the second or fighting stage of their development, they work very hard to rebuild their own ego at a stronger level. They fight realistic battle scenes with very real noises. Some boys tell me when they are through with this second phase by simply explaining they are tired of wars. Then they start making working-type scenes with much construction and movement going on. This, I feel, is the beginning of the third, or adaptive to the collective, stage for the boys.

At the third stage of development, the girls make scenes quite like the boys, also with much movement of cars and trucks, as well as construction. But the girls set up more familial patterns and construct more communities or towns. They also show very feminine symbols in their later stages of development, such as wombs and breasts. One feels they are now beginning to understand their own connection to life and the community through relationships. Boys show masculine and feminine sexual symbols too. However, I notice boys use these symbols, if at all, at any stage, whereas girls begin to use them more at the third or later stages. Both boys and girls make very creative scenes at this time, and begin to feel like separate and complete individuals.

Whether it is a boy or a girl, it is always exciting and deeply meaningful for me when I know that the child feels connected and is ready for separation. Each individual must walk his own path, and that is a wonderful feeling to share at the right moment.

I have finished my book, yet I still ask: does the owl really teach the child wisdom of the outer world? Does the bear really teach us how to think from the inside? Do birds teach inner power and little mice keep us humble and grounded to earth? These mysterious forces wind their ways into the development process, leaving books and categories and labels in a position of offering limited explanations. What happens in sandplay therapy is as mysterious as life itself, defying descriptions and labels. And the final turn of the screw is that the one who is being analyzed is the only one who knows the answer. As one child said: "I traveled and found someone else's gold. I traveled some more and found my own."

So I have chosen to tell about the children whose paths I feel illustrate aspects of sandplay at different ages and experience. I tell about the individuation journey of five different boys ranging in ages from nine to thirteen, and I describe the feminine way of three young girls. A fifth chapter describes sandplay therapy involving an adult, a person we will call Mary. In my last chapter I discuss two miniatures, the bear and owl, frequently chosen by many children for their sand pictures. I try to explain why these are used so often and how the healing process is aided by their frequent use. I describe their meanings and histories as they were known in past cultures, without stripping them of their mystery. The ultimate question is this: are we all searching for new symbols and deeper meanings for some of the old ones, just as the children and adults who work in sand are finding healing through the use of both the most archaic and the most contemporary of ideas and images?

The Individuation Journey

3

STRUGGLE WITH THE OPPOSITES

Once there was a little boy who was caught up and cut off in all his beautiful and horrible daydreams. He dreamed of power, of castles and forts which he could control. He liked his dream world, but this world had its price. He could not read and he had terrible nightmares. He had no friends, and that really hurt. And all the adults were always angry with him. From the inside of his dream world, he looked out on the adults in the real world and they seemed very far away and terrifying to him. He saw his mother, shouting and crying much of the time. He saw his father as a physical giant who shook his dream world, even though he appeared gentle to adults in everyday life.

The little boy realized that he was paying a terrible price for his dreams and his fantasies; so he started on a journey out of his dream world. He destroyed the debris and cut down the walls. Other people began to seem more real to him. He learned to love his mother and little sister, and fought the good fight to relate to his father. There is still a long journey ahead for this little boy, but he has fought long and hard to come out of his dream world, and now, at least, his feet are on solid ground. Now he is really on the road.

This is a story about Mark, a very real little boy who, at seven and a half, was a great puzzle to all the adults in his world. Mark had been in school for more than one year, but had not yet started to read. His parents were worried that he might be mentally retarded. They took Mark to a physician who told them that he was not, that there was nothing physically wrong, but that Mark needed psychological help. The physician suggested to Mark's parents that they bring him to see me.

I chose to tell Mark's story because he follows so clearly the stages of individuation as described by Mrs. Dora Kalff and as I discuss in the Introduction: (1) vegetative, or stasis; (2) fighting or struggle; and (3) adaptation to the collective or community. When I first met Mark he seemed to be already in the fighting or struggle phase. Like many children, however, he spiraled back and forth into the watery, vegetative or static stage.

I first began seeing Mark at a real crisis point in his life. At home one day, in a fit of temper, he had actually picked up a hoe and attacked a little girl. He had made no real friends at school, but sometimes managed to have enough influence over the other boys to get them to do the dangerous and destructive things he planned.

Mark seemed to need to fight or struggle very strongly, and perhaps this was partially because of the temporary split which had just occurred in his own family. Mark desperately needed to be close to his father, but he had just left the family to accept a good position in Spain. Although the family was to join him in Spain as soon as possible, the year of separation was very difficult for Mark. Mark's mother was Spanish and his father was American. The couple had met and married in Spain, and had come to the San Francisco Bay Area before the children were born.

Mark's fantasy world was a very strong one. It had very high walls which took a long time to break down, so Mark stayed in the struggle stage of development longer than most children. He fought hard and progressed quickly, however, and he was well into the third, or adaptation-to-the-community stage, when the family left to join the father in Spain, just one year after I started seeing Mark. He had started to relate to both his family and his peers in a most human way.

Mark and I got along well from the beginning. Not only was he enchanted with the sand, he was also excited about the idea of a grown lady actually spending her time playing in the sand with him. Right away, Mark seemed to trust the situation; he related me to a godmother of his who would also play games of fantasy with him. Mark often told this godmother about his painful and terrifying nightmares; she was the only other person whom Mark let into this secret and important world.

With the rest of his family, Mark was often very removed. He would go into his room, play with his blocks and toy castle for many hours and would not allow his family to enter. Inside his room, Mark built very high walls out of blocks for his castle. Outside, he made very strong forts that no one, he hoped, could push down.

Knowing this fact about Mark's behavior, I found it natural that his first sand picture was a scene of a castle with high walls (Figure 1). In making this picture, Mark wet the sand in a controlled way and packed and molded it with much patience. Although a few canals dug around the castle give some sense of openness to this picture, on the whole the mood is one of tightness and control, which is expressed quite clearly in the careful molding of the sand. As this was Mark's first sand picture, I studied it carefully. I could not help noticing the strong phallic thrust expressed in the shape of the castle's canals and towers.

FIGURE I

It took Mark nearly the whole hour to finish the first picture. In the limited time he had left, he insisted on going to the dry box, where he quickly dug out two deep vessel-like caves. He put boats in one of these, and army equipment and knights in the other. The cave, the hidden or secret place, was certainly the theme of this picture, as the tower or fortress was the theme of his first picture, although there were some dug-out canals in that one as well. It seemed then, that this second dry picture was a kind of complement to the first model of the castle (Figure 2). The castle was the strong fortress, the masculine side of fantasy. The caves were the hidden, magical, deep places, or the feminine womb side of fantasy. This type of strong, intense symbolism is unusual in children so young.

I was concerned by the fact that Mark needed to divide his fantasy so completely by making such different and separate sandboxes. On rare occasions a few children whom I had seen before had made two boxes, but not in the same way as Mark had done. I intuited that there might be some danger of an actual split in his emotional life, and that this split might be the real theme which was being expressed in the symbolism of the two boxes. As I got to know Mark

FIGURE 2

better, I realized that this intuition was correct, and that he was, in some ways, cut off from his own emotions and instinctual life.

On Mark's second visit, his picture seemed much less ominous to me than the first two. He includes some strong houses with families inside. Here Mark uses the American flag, an identity symbol, showing that he has some root and some center. Also, in this picture his walls are lower than the high, strong, tight walls of his first picture. There are still, however, many soldiers and much fighting equipment. Mark said he was riding in the strongest jeep.

On this second visit, Mark wanted to tell a story about his first two pictures, the one of the castle and the dug-outs. He told me that "Centuries and centuries ago, there was a castle with lots of men in it. The men were so unfortunate of enemies, and then, before they knew it, they were overrun with them. Men were running here and there. There were helicopters coming out of the clearies; they were being bombed down like everything, and there were other helicopters. The men were very glad because they had shot so many men and they wanted to end the war. They won the war. The End."

As this story shows, Mark was quite interested in fighting and violence, but he also wanted to end the war. Mark talked a great deal to me on this second visit, and when he was not talking, he was imitating every conceivable battle noise. Sometimes, he would keep up the airplane and war sounds for a half hour at a time.

Mark also shared a dream with me on this second visit. He dreamed he was trying to get on the train where his father was, but that his father would not let Mark come on board because the boy was too dirty. Mark then told me he had many monster nightmares. Often, before he went to sleep at night, he saw his father's shadow on the walls, looking like a huge giant. It seemed quite possible to me that Mark had actually seen his father's shadow cast on the wall when his father was at home. I knew how their house was constructed, and that Mark's bedroom was just off the kitchen. Obviously, Mark's father often had come to the kitchen near Mark's door late at night, and probably looked in to see if his son was sleeping. The light from the kitchen coming in through Mark's door would certainly have thrown strange shadows on his wall. Mark's father is a very tall man, so his shadow could easily have looked like the shadow of a giant to Mark.

I understood all of this, yet it still seemed puzzling to me that Mark should carry the heavy burden of his father's shadow in waking life as well. Mark never complained to me of anything his father might have done to him, but he always talked about how loudly his mother and little sister shouted, and ended up saying that he could shout louder than either one of them. As I came to know the family better, I realized that Mark carried his father's shadow because he was forced, unconsciously, by his mother and sister to take on the actual role of head of the family. Mark's little sister was very demanding and still got most of his mother's attention, while Mark was the recipient of much of his mother's frustration and anger.

I saw a humorous example of how Mark carried his father's shadow on his next visit to me. Mark came in wearing a slipper, saying he had hurt his foot. He was limping noticeably and said he was sure he would have to have crutches just like his father had. In fact, Mark's father had hurt his foot and had used crutches a short time before he left for Spain. I told Mark I was very sorry about his foot. When he asked if he could take off his slipper so the cool floor would make his foot feel better, I consented. Close to the end of the hour, Mark assured me his foot was all healed, and it was obvious that he was no longer limping. He said he felt sure my cool floor had cured him.

During this visit, Mark again used two sandtrays. He carried on war games between the two sandboxes, one filled with Arab soldiers, the other with knights. During this fourth session, Mark's little sister begged to come into our room and play in the sand for a while. I had mixed feelings about permitting Mark's sister to share his time with me, but Mark said that he would like it. So I allowed her to come in and use a sandtray. Still a very little girl—four and a half years old—all she did was place two large baby dolls in the sandbox, bury them in the sand, then dig them out again. When Mark finished his picture, he noticed what his sister was doing and became very angry with her. Pulling her dolls out of the sand, Mark scolded his sister: "You are not to do it that way!" Then, to show his sister how to properly use the sand, he quickly made a picture of a volcano. In Mark's scene, figures of people and soldiers, including some army equipment, were destroyed by the volcano. This scene quite clearly revealed some of Mark's submerged but explosive emotional feelings about his family.

On Mark's next visit, some of these deep and angry feelings were still evident. Still upset about his sister's sandplay, he told me she should not be allowed to play in the sand again. On this visit Mark again made a very large cavelike castle with high walls. As I started to mold a very small piece of one wall, Mark said, "Don't help. You know that adults are apt to destroy things." However, after he had carried on his usual war games and battle cries in his completed sand picture, Mark did something quite different (Figure 3). He carefully placed two doors against one side of his castle, and as he left the room he said to me, "You know that the doors can open." Then he smiled his beautiful quiet smile and left.

FIGURE 3

Mark again made two pictures in the sand on his sixth visit to me. His first picture, which he made in the form of a circle, was done in the wet sandbox (Figure 4). He called the circular formation a volcano. Animals and houses were placed inside the circle, in what Mark called the sides of the volcano. This scene is full of threatening and violent elements. Mark explained that, besides the volcano, there was a war going on between the Germans and the Americans.

After making this picture, Mark talked to me for a while about his fear of dogs. He also told me about his toy train. Remembering Mark's fearful dreams of trains and the feelings of separation and loneliness associated with them, I felt Mark was now expressing another one of his deep fears. Then Mark asked to use my bathroom, and stayed away for quite a while. When he came back, he said that he wanted to "bomb the sandbox." This did not surprise me too much in view of all that had been happening. I knew that Mark would have to destroy what he had made before he could create his own journey and separation. With much noise, he bombed each figure in the entire sandbox. He hesitated, however, before destroying the two strong figures of elephants he had placed in his scene so carefully. But he said at last, "They must die also."

FIGURE 4

Mark made another picture in the dry sandbox which at first I did not consider too carefully. He had not destroyed this one. After he left, I realized this picture was made in the form of an egg or circle, with three distinct sections. At the north or top of the picture (whenever possible, I will describe sand pictures as though the sandtray had a compass inside; where the subject stands is the south—however, many children move completely around the tray as they work), Mark placed a row of airplanes. In the center, he put figures of workmen digging the earth and constructing. At the south or bottom of the box he lined up some boats. The elemental, lifegiving images of sky, earth and water were all enclosed within the circle. One cannot help but feel that this is like a creation myth after the destruction and chaos of the scene before. After a child destroys a sand picture, the next creation is always very important, for it will express the child's reaction to his own destruction. It symbolizes what is to be renewed after the old ego is destroyed. In Mark's case the high walls of his castle came down so he could face his world with more confidence.

On his next visit to me, Mark made a picture which seemed to have a real significance for him (Figure 5). When I studied my photograph of this scene, the entire format of the sand picture looked like a person, with a head, a body, and outstretched arms. The arms of the figure were wide, and they stretched out far, so that the entire figure could be a snow angel. After the destruction of his last picture it seemed that Mark, in this production, was definitely rebuilding his own ego or body. The figure of the person certainly symbolized Mark's need to find himself as a person, to find his own basic nature and to use that nature as a base for building his life.

This picture, like many of Mark's other scenes, is still full of symbols of war and violence, but it also has many elements standing for protected places and identity symbols. The feet of his figure, according to which the entire model is shaped, contain soldiers and horses seeking protection. They are moving towards a very strong fort, constructed inside that part of the figure which looks like the trunk, or middle part of the body. This fort is very well-protected. A canal encircles it, and two guards stand at lookout outside.

Near the northern part of the sandbox, inside the "head" of the figure, is the site of the battle being depicted in the box. It is interesting that Mark chose to use the head part of his figure for an area depicting war and fighting. He seemed to realize, in a symbolic sense, that his own battles must be fought and won in his mind. Although there is much confusion and fighting in this war scene, some positive symbols emerge in this area of the picture. For example, each small group of fighting soldiers carries its own flag as an identity symbol. Although they are fighting, the soldiers still know who they are and where they come from. It seems Mark realizes that through the battles being fought inside of his own mind, he will

FIGURE 5

eventually find a reliable and stable sense of identity.

More fighting men, with horses and equipment, are placed above and below the arms of the figure formed by the sand. These men, however, are not engaged in battle. Rather, they are protected behind stout walls. If the arms of the figure represent the ability to give and receive affection, to reach out and really touch others, it seems that Mark himself is still afraid to reach out to others, that he still keeps himself heavily defended by not showing his need for love. Yet in this part of the picture there is one soldier who is not hiding. This soldier seems to be a leader, or commander, as he is moving out of one of the fortresses and carrying a flag with a gesture that looks almost like a surrender. It seems that, on some level, Mark is admitting to himself that he needs to be close to other people, that he is getting ready to break down some of his own fortress walls and to surrender to this need.

After constructing this picture, Mark talked about his earlier picture of a volcano, and quietly stated, "It had to be destroyed." I felt I knew he meant that this picture represented fears that had been holding him back from full participation in life. Those walls had to be broken down in order for him to use his fantasy life in a more constructive way.

My feeling was strengthened by Mark's second quick picture in the dry box. He had asked me to help him place the box closer to the very intricate scene in the wet box. When the slide was taken, this picture looked very much like a Christmas creche, probably because it was behind the other picture. In fact, it is not too different, at least symbolically. Mark had made a small fort with four sides and then elongated it by using the walls of the fort for the fifth side. He then carefully placed five soldiers and horses inside, saying this was their secret hiding place, and made a hidden cave for the men and horses. The symbols of the cave, the hidden place, the five walls and the five men, cannot be explained or interpreted rationally, nor do I wish to do so.

On Mark's next visit to me, he made a sand picture which expressed more fully his search for identity and independence. While making this picture, Mark first scooped out a shallow cave in the sand which looked quite like a womb. He then carefully placed army equipment inside this cave for protection. In the center west, he dug another small cave and put a fence in front of it. He put the figure of a little girl inside. I thought at first this little girl was a prisoner, but Mark assured me she was being protected, not imprisoned. It seemed thus obvious to me that the little girl represented the childlike but independent side of Mark's own nature which still needed to be protected as it developed. Strangely, Mark named this picture "Naomi Land"—Naomi is a Biblical name meaning "I and Me."

Protection and security are certainly the themes of this picture. It is interesting that Mark brings in all three basic elements—air, earth, and water—representing them by the airplanes, land forces, and submarines, respectively. Apparently, all were to ensure the security of the little girl. "She must be protected," Mark explained to me. Here, it seemed, Mark was beginning to realize that he was more than just his father's shadow, that he was a person in his own right. Mark was also beginning to realize that he no longer had to build walls high enough to keep out all the world. He could tear down some of his walls completely, and let the real Mark go more openly and honestly into a world without so many scary shadows.

Mark now also seemed to become less compelled by violence. On his tenth visit, he talked, as usual, of war, but he also talked more about his school, a private one which was "free" or, more negatively stated, one with a permissive environment. Mark told me that when his own children grew up he would provide them with helmets and earplugs so they would not have to hear all the dirty words and noises continually going on in schools.

On this visit, Mark made a sand picture depicting a protected and secure island (Figure 6). The large bridge, one of the most striking elements in the picture, is well protected by airplanes at its southeast end, and, in the center of the picture, by a gate guarded by two soldiers on the bridge leading onto the island. The island itself, surrounded by a deep moat and encircled by a wall, contains a large house and a storeroom fort also protected by soldiers and military equipment. Inside the walled island, much movement and life is represented by many figures of horses and people. The last thing Mark placed in the southwest corner of the sandbox was a towerlike Christmas creche. Looking at the entire picture, one can see a circle within the square of the sandbox itself—that is, a mandala. A very open and patiently made mandala, it has small openings (which Mark called windows) along the outside of the smaller circle. The wide, deep moat seems to add security to the entire picture. Since a circle or mandala is the projected image of the person making the picture, I feel this lovely picture showed a real spiral development in Mark's life and journey. Order and unity were definitely evolving from the chaos of his earlier life.

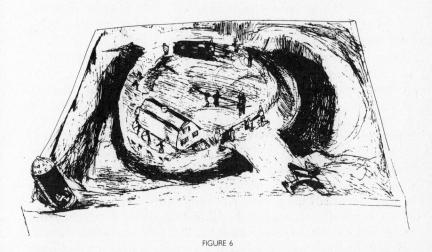

FIGURE 6

When Mark asked if he could bring a friend to his next session to play in the sand, I recognized this as yet a further indication of his increasingly open attitude toward other people. Although I rarely allow this, I consented.

At the next session, much was accomplished in terms of harmonious mutual play and understanding between Mark and his friend. I was very glad I had consented to the other boy's participation in the session. From the beginning, both became totally absorbed in their creations in separate sandboxes. Mark made a picture similar to some he had made previously. He carefully built a castle with moats and turrets surrounding it. He then built a smaller castle out of sand and placed it inside the larger one.

Mark's friend chose Noah's ark, placing it in the middle of his sandbox. He then filled the ark with animals and people and proceeded to cover it up with sand. He covered and uncovered the inside of the ark many times. Mark, after finishing his picture, saw his friend burying animals and the ark. Obviously unhappy with his friend's activities, Mark told him the story of Noah and the flood, emphasizing the theme of the deluge and salvation which are so much a part of that story. He told how Noah carefully picked two animals of each species, placed them in the ark to save them from the flood, and then how Noah searched for land, for some sign that the flood was over and life could begin anew. Impressed with Mark's knowledge of the story, his friend immediately stopped burying the figures.

After Mark told Noah's story, he helped his friend rebuild the scene. The boys paired off all of the animal figures and placed them in a line as if they were entering the ark. One of them took the figure of a young boy and placed it on the roof of the ark, saying that the boy was looking out for land.

The boys then wanted to put their two sand pictures together, and asked me to help them to move the two boxes (Figure 7). When this was done, they built a large wooden bridge connecting the two boxes. This bridge seemed to signal a deep and final connection for Mark, a path from his inner fantasy world to the world outside. After connecting the bridge to his friend's picture, Mark never needed to make two divided sand scenes again. After this, he would either put two boxes close together or work in just one box. Mark's increasing sense of connection to the world seemed to be confirmed by the fact that he was finally beginning to read a little.

In his next few sessions, Mark made more battle scenes, but now these included more playful elements than did his earlier war pictures. In one session, he asked if his sister could come with him once more. When he brought her on his next visit, they worked well in the sand together. Mark finished his picture before his sister finished hers, but this time was content with just giving her some gentle instructions about not burying her dolls in the sandbox. He then helped her complete her scene, placing a large house with a flowerpot on its roof, and people and children all around it. As he worked, he said: "Let's make it a family." Together they appeared to be very much a family as they left talking quietly and laughing.

During this session, Mark made a much more complex picture than the one of the house and family he had built with his sister. Although another war scene, it seemed to have more to with the

FIGURE 7

beauties of nature than with war, with deep, spiraled canals and waterways covering most of the box. About this picture, Mark said, "The ocean is stirred up and coming to land."

It seemed that the peaceful rhythm of water was now part of Mark's life, and this serenity showed in his work with me. He no longer seemed to need the box to portray violent scenes of battle. Sometimes he would just create a small, peaceful scene in the dry box. Once, he traced a face in the dry sand.

Mark's life outside of treatment was also more peaceful. His reading was progressing fairly well, and he was making quite a few friends at school. I knew that Mark was now learning to control his desire to fight. He was moving out of the fighting stage of his development into a more adaptive, community stage of growth. During one of his last visits, Mark made a picture of a fort with soldiers guarding it. Although it was a little like some of his other war pictures, it was different because the war equipment used was there to *prevent* violence. Mark placed two jeeps, or trucks, in the center saying: "These are special trucks because they drain off debris, and hold the volcano back from too much destruction."

On another visit, he made a scene in the shape of a circle, saying that it was the site of a new hospital; the flowers and trees inside the circle seem to show a concern for healing and for beauty I had never seen Mark feel free enough to demonstrate before. Mark had never used flowers, trees, or any greenery in any of his previous pictures.

When he next came to see me, Mark made another partial war scene. However, there is much less war equipment in this scene, and much more hand-to-hand combat. And he included a house, something rarely included in war scenes. Mark called it the King's house. At first he said that a volcano would destroy this king's house, but then he said, "No, let it stand." In context of his previous pictures, this picture, containing the threat of violence, showed me that Mark was really progressing through the fighting and struggle stage into an integrated or adaptation-to-the-community stage of development.

Mark made two more pictures before he ended his treatment and, with his mother and sister, joined his father in Spain. His last picture seemed a very hopeful one to me, telling of his growing integration, and of the increasing inclusion of beauty into his world (Figure 8). During this last session, we were both somewhat quiet and serious because we knew we were parting. I was leaving for a holiday and he for Spain, so I did not pay as close attention to the picture Mark was making as I usually did.

FIGURE 8

After Mark left, I was deeply moved by the beautiful bull-fighting arena he had made. This picture, like his others, combined elements of violence with more peaceful themes. To the north of the arena is a man feeding animals from a cart. This small scene balances and offsets the scene of destruction of animals which, one imagines, would be taking place in the arena, along with the emotional outpouring inherent in that spectacle. Mark included some figures which also had a religious connotation. To the right or western side of the arena, he placed the figures of Joseph, Mary and Jesus as a family leaving Bethlehem, with Mary and Jesus on the back of a donkey, and Joseph leading them. Mark had made a quiet and peaceful road for Jesus' family. Remembering that Mark was to travel with his own family soon, the imagery of the Holy Family moving out of Bethlehem seemed all the more remarkable. Symbolically, I was sure that Mark had started on his own inner journey as well.

Mark made another simple scene in the dry sandbox. He made a semi-circle of houses with the church in the center, and then placed a number of white Arabs around in the sand, along with their horses and camels. We talked a bit about this because he said he was worried about the fact that his mother was not interested in religion. He had mentioned this before. He told me they were fighting over the church. As he left what we thought was his last visit, he said to his mother: "It's really sad to say goodbye to friends."

In these last two pictures it seemed to me that Mark was making a real connection between struggle and serenity, both in the outside world as he saw it and his own interior world. At this time too, after I had left on holiday, his godmother wrote me that Mark had shared a dream with her and asked her to tell me about it. The godmother wrote, "Mark is finding the gates through this rather high wall that seems mossy and unattractive. It is very difficult to get through, but when he does succeed, he finds a beautiful garden. There is also a house for the chickens. In the center it's like a temple or throne surrounded by flowers."

Indeed, for Mark at this point the end of the ugly fighting seems to have led to a peaceful and beautiful place. I am glad there is a house for the chickens, needed elements in life. Mark at least has seen this beautiful garden and is less fearful of the outside world. He is bringing down the castle walls and meeting a world rich in relationships, a world of blooming gardens but also of ordinary chicken debris—a living world.

Mark is a wonderfully intelligent and expressive boy, and he has other qualities just as important as intelligence. He is a great dreamer, a dreamer who knows how to translate the language of his dreams into everyday words and actions which will make up the substance of his life. The sandbox pictures he made helped him express this interior language and to understand and respect it. Mark was able to really communicate some of the elements of his dream world to me through the medium of the sandtray. Once he had communicated and understood his fantasies, there was no reason to hide behind them anymore. Perhaps as a result of the change in Mark's behavior, Mark's entire family became closer and more communicative, a circumstance that helped Mark to break down even more of his defensive walls. Today, Mark is in a good state of communication with both his own interior world of symbols and dreams, and with the outside world, with other people. His teacher gives me good reports of his progress. Time alone will tell whether Mark will be able to maintain this balance in his life.

The sandtray gave Mark an opportunity to act out and live through his dreams and fantasies. I feel that sandplay was the medium through which he established a truly durable connection with his interior world, a bridge which should help him greatly throughout his life.

4

FINDING ONE'S OWN WORTH

John's parents came to see me in desperation because their oldest son was, quite suddenly, unable to do his schoolwork and nearly failing his classes. Physical illness aggravated this situation; almost every morning, John became nauseated and vomited. He was often so ill that he could not attend classes. His parents said John had been thoroughly checked by his doctor. Although John had suffered from some fairly severe stomach ailments, his doctor could see no physical reason for these recent problems. Because John was also having frequent nightmares, the physician suggested John's parents contact me for psychological help.

When I first saw John, I was struck by his size: he was very small for a boy of nine. His size seemed to disturb John as well, since his family was composed of physically large and strong people. His father, an athletic man, was a probation officer. John's brother (seven) and sister (five) were both very large children. The younger brother was actually taller and heavier than John. These early observations of size gave me a clue as to why John might feel threatened and upset. John's parents seemed to strongly emphasize school performance and wanted the children to succeed academically. This desire was so strong they moved the family to a rather exclusive suburban community. Although they could barely afford living in this suburb, they continued to feel it most important to maintain a residence there and send their children to what they considered superior suburban schools. Knowing all this, I could understand why John felt pressure from his parents to do well in his schoolwork.

But there were also many positive facets to John's family life. As a Catholic family, they kept close to each other with their shared religious faith and belief in family life. John's parents were genuinely concerned with all the children and willing to make financial sacrifices to help them, even with another baby on the way and very little money to spare.

When John's parents recognized how well he related to me from the outset, they gave all the emotional and financial support they could to John and his therapy. Actually, they did seem to expect miracles from me. When a dramatic change does occur in a relatively short time, as in John's case, a rational explanation is not always possible. I have worked with the sandtray long enough now to respect the mystery of the healing process and to not question the inner healing mechanism of the psyche.

John worked well in the sandtray from the beginning. His first picture was full of interesting and meaningful symbols, but he did not want to talk about them very much. He simply said the picture represented "a war between the cowboys and the Indians" (Figure 9). To me, the picture represented much more, but I respected John's silence, feeling that we would come to understand the deeper meaning of some of John's symbols in the course of his therapy.

FIGURE 9

Although John passed over the significance of this picture with the one casual remark, he seemed to feel the importance of the picture as he built it; he put much effort into constructing the fort just right and placing it carefully toward the exact bottom center of his picture. The fort had four strongposts or lookout towers. John put people, horses and supplies inside the fort. The supplies included a large black cooking pot placed in a central part of the fort. On the left or west side of the fort was a river with a boat bringing more people and supplies to the fort. Indians were attacking the fort from the north.

At the very top of the box, John made a different scene using knights and a castle. The knights approach the castle on a road, as if trying to get inside. In the center of the picture, John had a meeting among the knights, the cowboys and the Indians. Four horsemen, including two knights, an Indian and a cowboy, rode in a circular path. Some shrubs and trees were placed to the right or east of these circling riders.

In the northeastern corner of the sandtray, John carefully created a very realistic scene of a man being hung on the gallows. He colored the hanged man with red crayon to show blood and took great trouble in making a noose which looked very real. Unfortunately, the slide does not show this noose too clearly, but it was frighteningly realistic.

The last thing John did was place a large, plastic black-widow spider on the roof of the supply house inside the fort. The spider seemed to me an important symbol even though John did not talk about it until later in therapy. It seemed important to honor John's silence, and I felt the meaning of the spider would soon be clear to him. The very realistic figure of the hanged man told me how very threatened John felt at this time; words were not necessary.

Because there were also many positive elements in this first picture, I had a good feeling about John's treatment from the outset. The secure fort emanated much energy and life; the horsemen, riding out of the fort and the castle and circling around the center, gave the feeling of reaching out for adventure from a place of security. John showed great honesty and awareness of his feelings when he depicted the hanged man, a dangerous and threatening image.

I was puzzled, however, by the meaning of some of the symbols in the picture, especially the spider, so I began to look into John's external world more closely.

As I mentioned, John was the older and smaller of the two boys in his family. His father, who was large and strong, expressed a great interest in sports. Thus John felt threatened just by virtue of his size and relative lack of competitive athletic ability. He worried slightly about the new baby on the way. Undoubtedly, he wondered whether this baby would take even more of his parents' time and attention away from himself.

Things were no better for John at school. I met his teacher, a large, rather overbearing woman. She expressed concern about John's lack of academic progress in a rather aggressive way. She said John "could not or would not read" in a way that showed all her own frustrations and disappointments in this situation. I was sure she must have communicated some of this disappointment and frustration to John. After getting to know this teacher I was able to better interpret the meaning of the black widow spider as a threatening feminine symbol to John. Once I thought about John's position in his family, his own mother heavy with a new life inside, and his situation at school, I did not find it at all surprising that this boy felt insecure and unhappy when he came to me.

John called his second significant scene a "desert scene." He commented mainly on the right or east side of this picture, where he placed several large elephants fighting a big cobra snake close by. John said: "The snake will bite the blue-gray elephant because he cannot read." When I looked at John, I could see his eyes were smiling a little, so it seemed all right to laugh with him for a bit. John was beginning to show his marvelous sense of humor, which shone through even in his depressed state.

He put many other animals in the desert scene, including, appropriately, camels as well as prehistoric mammals and birds. At the south end of the box, he placed some of the same large, colorful knight figures, as well as the place of protection and security he had used in his earlier "fort" picture. This time John used a clay cave in the northeastern corner of the box. He placed some nice pieces of driftwood in front of the cave. There was, however, a small, crawly-looking crab near the opening of the cave.

Toward the north end and in the center of the box, John made another realistic hanging scene very similar in violence to his first hanging man. He also did not neglect to put the black widow spider down in the sand, this time amidst the fighting knights and the fighting elephants in the south center of the box. All John's usual threatening and dangerous symbols were again present.

However, there were also some very positive elements in this sand scene. The lower western side is almost devoid of figures, except for the procession of three camels riding from the east and a man on horseback accompanying them. This procession had a very positive significance for me. First, it suggested the religious theme of the three wise men in the Christmas story, and I knew how important religion was to John. Second, it suggested that, even amidst all of the fighting and death, there were still animals who were strong enough to survive, and survive peacefully in the desert. Perhaps the connection I made to religious faith had something to do with this inner peaceful strength which seemed to be emanating from a natural place near the center of his sand scene. Paradoxically, I felt one of the strongest elements of this picture was one that clearly and visibly expressed fighting: a large, red catapult in the southeast corner. Unfortunately, the catapult is difficult to see in my illustration.

I remember quite clearly how John kept shooting arrows from this catapult and shouting his battle cries. He carried on a very realistic battle from the catapult, even showing the red wheels of a cart being struck by arrows, at the furthest or northern end of the sandbox. John became very involved in this battle. I felt that the red catapult and red cart wheels symbolized quite well John's passionate and lively emotions, which he so desperately needed to release at this time; it was safe to have the red machine do the actual fighting for him.

On one of John's visits, we finally talked about the black-widow spider. He seemed to know a lot about this insect and about the deadly and clinging power of the female of the species. Just talking about spiders seemed to help John to get over some of his negative and oppressive feelings. Soon after this talk, his mother called to say John had suddenly stopped having his horribly frightening nightmares. She also said John was very rarely ill in the mornings anymore.

John seemed to be more relaxed even with me after our talk about spiders. Once he brought his guitar and played and sang for me. On this visit, we talked a little about his nightmares, and John said, again with his wonderful sense of humor, that he felt some of his bad dreams had come from watching too many King Kong movies on television.

Accordingly, John made his last sand picture "to pen up King Kong." He showed this by placing two bears and a tiger in a large fenced-off pen in the northwestern corner of his picture. Near this pen, on its western side, John put some army jeeps, some fighting equipment, and a few trucks. Perhaps these vehicles were put there to guard the animals.

At the northern end of the sandtray, John placed two houses and built a road between them which extended down the entire western side of the sandtray. He called this road "a landing strip for airplanes" and showed one plane coming in for a landing. This landing strip symbol was very significant for John. It indicated that the healing process was taking place and that John, like the airplane, had a place to land, a place to come home to. The landing strip seemed to show that John was developing within himself a stable center, a place he could trust. The plane had crashed into a house before it landed, but John assured me the trucks and equipment he had put in the picture had mended all the damage. This story of the plane crashing into the house yet surviving told me something of John's own growing feelings of confidence in himself. Like the airplane, he had had some difficult and maybe even dangerous times but he could still land securely. The house might symbolize his own family and himself: they had been upset, as had he, but the damage was repaired and the house still stood.

Near the landing strip, John placed a most interesting stone or rock standing alone. Like the camel, this rock perhaps showed his ability to stand alone, or separate, to be strong and to survive. The rock is a very common religious symbol of the self.

The rest of this picture is filled with houses; to the center and south of the sandtray, one house stands unfinished. There are several trucks and men working on the construction of these houses. John even laid out some piping, to be connected for sewers and water, he said. Here he showed an awareness that we must always be connected to even the ugly side of life and not forget our source, water. The fact that the houses were being built at all showed movement and life in John, and a sense of new beginnings.

This picture contained no seriously frightening elements. John left out both the black-widow spider and the hanged man. This picture told me quite clearly that John had made peace with his destructive and fearful side. He seemed to have pulled himself together and made a good start on the journey of his life. He had moved from a paralyzing and frozen place to a central rock or stone. Life was moving for him.

After making this picture, John did not come to see me again for treatment, but I kept in touch with him and his parents regularly for the next two years. John was doing extremely well. He had accepted his small size and now had many friends. His parents told me about his fine sense of humor at home and how it kept the family in balance. John's mother had had a healthy baby girl, and John seemed to love the new baby and to take an interest in helping to care for her.

John's healing was so quick and so seemingly complete that it did seem like a miracle. I do believe in miracles, because I have seen them really happen. With the help of the sandtray and a sheltered place, both children and adults can make a needed connection with their own inner psychic energy or self, and encourage healing to take place.

Perhaps the real miracle is that healing is not only a straight road but moves two ways—for the healer as well as the one who comes for healing.

I am fortunate indeed to know some of the power and mystery of the everrenewing flow. Yes, the rock must be steady and grounded in the earth that needs to be watered at times; but the plane may fly to the sky and return, and the heart may be rent with fire and emotion, yet return to its steady beat. Life connected to living symbols does not stagnate for long; to all who take the time to listen, children will invariably say: "That is the straight of it."

5

LIVING ONE'S OWN MYTH

In this section, I want to tell the story of a boy who improved both his relationship with his group and his schoolwork. Despite very serious problems, he made tremendous strides with sandtray therapy. Although Bob's story is a success story, that is not why I relate it. I believe Bob's story can help explain the often miraculous changes that occur when people work with the sandtray and begin to relate to its healing symbols.

Bob first came to me when he was six and a half years old, and stayed until he was nearly nine. His physical problems were diagnosed in his medical report as minimal brain dysfunction with gross muscle involvement. Bob handled this medical problem by "acting out" his frustrations in silently aggressive ways. A rather large boy, Bob would physically attack his peers without warning. Although he had never seriously hurt anyone, his classmates feared him very much and the situation in the classroom became very tense.

The tension Bob created at school also appeared at home, as his behavior embarrassed his family. His two sisters, one a year younger than Bob and the other in her early teens, were especially affected by his behavior. Wanting to be socially accepted, both girls were embarrassed by Bob's sometimes violent behavior and preferred to have nothing to do with him.

Looking back, it is easy to understand why Bob seemed so frightened of the sandtray in the beginning and why he would just stick a few animals all around the tray and then ask if I had anything to eat in my house. It is interesting to note that the animals he chose for his first sandtray were an owl, three horses, three bears, lions, two tigers and two dogs.

To this day, I do not know how Bob found such a descriptive way to share such an important picture when he made his second scene in the sand. I am sure he does not know the "how" of it either. But we both know how it was necessary for him to express to me, with this picture, his deep fear of a monster he kept locked inside his own self. He even denied having monster dreams at this time.

With a little imagination, one can see in Bob's picture (Figure 10) a very real monster, a monster which seemed to be drowning and smothering the boy. The very wet, almost "globby" sand resembles an inhuman face. The two jeeps are eyes; the troop carrier, the nose; and the submarine, the mouth. The mass would be a sort of floating island if it were not connected to the rest of the land outside by a kind of hat at the top. This scene calls to mind the picture of an embryo surrounded by the waters of the mother and connected by the umbilical cord to the mother's body. Without this umbilical connection, the embryo could not be nourished.

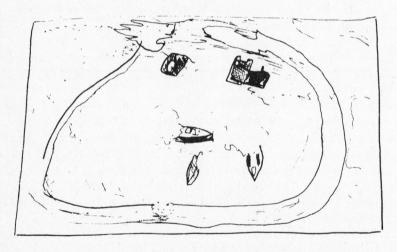

FIGURE 10

This picture made it clear to me that the work with Bob would be difficult. But the monster being connected by a sort of bridge to the rest of the sand, or land, made me hopeful that Bob, too, was still reaching out for nourishment and had not yet destroyed his bridge, both conscious and unconscious, to the rest of the world. At the same time, I knew Bob would not have an easy journey through his difficulties; and I felt that the journey would be difficult for me as well.

Bob and I worked well together. I was convinced of our progress a few weeks later when he made another important picture (Figure 11). This time, Bob shaped the sand in the center into a figure that looked very much like a large boat or ship. Instead of being submerged in water, as the monster was, the boat was partially stuck to the drier land. Bob placed a castle and a Chinese shrine inside the boat. Two bridges led from the boat to the dry sand, one on the south and one on the east. Bob then put two lighted candles in the center south, directly in front of one of the bridges. Finally he placed the church in the southwest corner.

FIGURE 11

Because Bob talked so little at first, it was difficult to know what he felt about the figures he chose. I certainly felt that the lighted candles introduced an element of hope not present in the earlier monster picture. The candles seemed to say that as we worked together, the way of his journey would come to light. Church seemed important to Bob, and he talked about this but confessed that the kids teased him a lot in church school. He placed the castle, a figure he used often in his later pictures, in the center with the Chinese shrine close by. This seemed meaningful to him, and I felt very positive about all his choices. While a castle can mean many things, to most children it represents at least a secret place where they can be safe. They also think of it as being very old and durable.

Bob flooded the sand over and over again. Sometimes he would fill the whole tray with water and have boats and mountains floating around. At other times, he would put figures of soldiers, horses and equipment in the tray and then almost drown them with water.

It was a real chore for me to dry out the tray and the sand, and it certainly made me feel that I was earning my money. Bob was rather excessive with me in other ways, too, and we had to set and enforce a few limits on his behavior.

Bob liked to use clay, but he could never stick with it long enough for anything to be completed. He kept trying, though, telling me how good he was at making things. He also liked to paint, and about ten months after he started seeing me, he painted an eight-pronged cross. The colors in the painting (Figure 12) were predominantly gold and green with some red-orange and a small amount of black. The choice of colors, gold, green and orange, seemed to be warm and perhaps cleansing for Bob. A square frame enclosed the entire cross. Again, I felt that Bob's work had a deep significance for him, but that it would take some time for him to realize the deeper meaning of his own symbols. At this stage, it was a new experience for him to keep one of his paintings and not smear or destroy it before others saw it.

FIGURE 12

This painting showed another side of Bob, helping me understand his confusion about his own identity. To my mind, Bob's intuitive, almost delicate inner nature came out clearly in this picture. He had been seeing me long enough now to feel free to show me his wonderful sweet and tender nature. But to the world outside, he still showed only his aggressive and hostile feelings. Still physically aggressive around his sisters and his classmates, he was generally regarded as a "bad guy." But the sandtray pictures and the paintings helped him get in touch with energy from his own unconscious. He began to communicate some of his inner psyche to me. He smiled and talked more often about school and home.

I called Bob's next sand picture (Figure 13) "the destruction of dead gods," because it really marked a change in him. Just making this picture seemed to help Bob drop some old, unproductive ways of adapting and to adopt some new and more productive patterns of behavior. Bob himself called the figures that he chose "old gods." These figures were carvings other children and I had made using clay or plaster of Paris: there was something mysterious and otherworldly about them. Bob arranged these figures around the tray with a few trees, flowers and pieces of driftwood. He even placed the figure of a mountain goat on top of a white statue.

Then Bob did something I found very interesting. He asked if he could melt some paraffin he had already colored with crayons. He poured the melted wax in the tray and stuck a small, gray plastic soldier in the center of the puddle before it hardened. This wax puddle looked like a head or face, and it was very dark, almost black in color.

FIGURE 13

The completed picture shows the white god statue, with the mountain goat placed on top of it, in the center and north part of the sandtray. Directly to the left or west of the white statue is a clay piece that also looks very much like a green face; Bob placed a flower close by. To the right or east of the white god, and more toward tne front of the tray, Bob left his puddle of wax with the small plastic soldier or knight standing up in the middle of it. Bob placed driftwood and flowers around this soldier, making the whole figure resemble a head even more, since this arrangement looked somewhat like hair. It may be possible that the aggressive soldier had to die. Death by fire is certainly destructive, but it is also cleansing or clearing. Bob told me later he was attempting to make a sand candle.

From this time on, fire became an important element in all of Bob's pictures. At first, this was a bit scary, because Bob used fire quite extensively. But I felt he was entering a new and productive stage for him: using fire, he was symbolically moving away from water and on to a more feeling element in his life.

Bob made volcanoes in the sand and lit papers inside them, leaving a hole in the mountain so the papers drew enough air to burn. When he asked if he could burn some papers in my wastebasket, I did say no. After this, we talked about the creative and destructive possibilities of fire. Perhaps it was fortunate for my own peace of mind that Bob's parents had neglected to tell me that he had once nearly set their entire home on fire by carelessly playing with matches.

After Bob had made many pictures full of volcanic fires, he made a very different kind of picture in the sand (Figure 14). He placed

FIGURE 14

two army jeeps and a candle in the center of the sandtray; then he asked for several small books of matches. He then placed an army tank on one side of the sandtray and an army cannon on the other side, and then began, very patiently, to pull every match out of the books. He stuck these matches in the sand to form a circle with the candle and jeeps as its center, leaving the cannon and tank as part of the outer circle. At this point, I really had no idea of what he intended to do, but I realized that it was most important to him.

Bob said very little until he lit the candle in the center. Then he insisted I get my camera ready to take a picture, because he was going to light each match and get the entire circle of matches burning at once. I didn't really believe he could do this, but I watched him work carefully and quickly and get the entire circle burning at the same time. As the matches started to go out, I realized I must take the picture quickly. The slide shows many of the matches still burning.

I felt as though I had observed an actual ritual. When I looked at the slide later, I saw a ring of fire. I remembered the graceful and careful way that Bob had ignited the matches in succession to produce this effect, and this thought made me realize that Bob had at last contained his own inner fire. He had used fire in an active and creative way by engaging in a sort of self-created rite.

Whatever the meaning of this ritual, it marked the end of Bob's need to make destructive fires with me. At about this time, Bob's

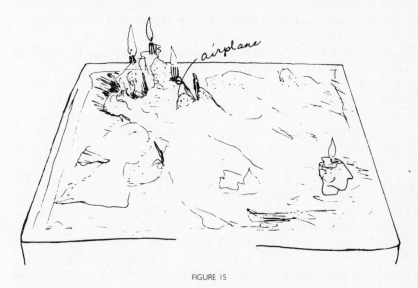

FIGURE 15

parents mentioned the fact that he had once almost burned down their house by accident. They had noticed that recently he had become more trustworthy with matches, and they were now letting him help with lighting the fireplace and home barbecues. They asked me why Bob had changed, but I felt the time was not yet right to share the "ring of fire" story with them.

Bob continued to use lighted candles and matches in his pictures, but more sparingly. One of these later sand scenes (Figure 15), which seemed especially significant, had a volcano erupting and watery lava flowing down its sides. There were caverns in the mountainside, through one of which Bob somehow managed to make a lighted candle shine. He then asked for four more candles; I only had three, so Bob used a piece of wax stuck to the top of a male figurine as his fourth candle. He put the man's head at the bottom of the lava, behind the other three candles he had lit and placed atop the mountain; he put his favorite airplane nearby. He seemed to be saying that out of the three lights and the destruction of the volcano had come the fourth light. In other words, the man's head emerged as representing maturity—i.e., out of destruction shall come light.

In his outer life, Bob began to think through his destructive impulses and to use this energy in a more constructive way. Although good reports came back from his school, it takes a long time to reverse a bad reputation. Bob seemed to understand that much in his life still needed to be settled, and that it would take much time before this process were completed. This awareness may explain the continuing volcanic eruptions and scenes of destruction in his pictures. However, his scenes certainly showed more containment.

Now Bob no longer needed to flood the sandtray. He made a picture a few weeks later, a small mountain which he flattened into a plateau; he placed his favorite castle at its center. In the far northwest corner he molded some hills and placed some trees. He dug a moat all around the mountain and filled it with water. The water was as carefully contained in this picture as the fire in the "ring of fire" picture. Bob put a sailboat in the water on the northeast side of the mountain. Spanning the southeastern side of the moat was a strong bridge made of sand. He modeled the bridge more smoothly and carefully than anything he had made before. The bridge was also a hopeful symbol to me, as it always seems to denote communication or reaching out.

After making the "ring of fire" and the moat pictures, Bob seemed to be able to play freely in the sand and to enjoy himself doing so. He seemed to have overcome his desire to flood and burn the tray; he had used the elements of fire and water constructively and creatively. Now he would fill the sandtray with engines, cars, and trucks riding along curving roads (Figure 16). On one visit he brought a big truck from home to try out on the roads he made.

On one of his later visits, Bob startled me when he brought his pet rat and said he wanted it to play in the sand, too. I said, "No, he can't," and of course Bob asked me for a reason. I first I tried to explain politely, but I should have known better. Bob wanted to test me and pretended that he did not understand my explanation. So I just said, "I like your pet rat, but I won't let him pee in our sandtray." I had never heard Bob laugh as heartily as he did

FIGURE 16

then; he quickly put his rat back in its cage and we both enjoyed the rest of the hour.

At this time, Bob was completing his second school year since he had been in treatment with me. I was going on vacation, and although we both looked forward to a break we promised to send each other postcards. His last picture before vacation made me feel that all would eventually go well with Bob despite the many ups and downs he might continue to experience in his life.

Bob simply called the picture "a landing strip for airplanes." He actually made two landing strips, using fences laid down flat on the sand. He put two trees between the strips, on a palm tree with what he called a "monkey-god" on one of its branches, the other an oak tree. He placed his favorite plane between the landing strips. Then he carefully lit five matches and put them at the end of one of the strips, as lights for the landing field. The complete picture shows the two trees on the left or west side, one airstrip in the center, and one on the right or east side. The airplane is coming in from east to west.

I was quite pleased with the image he chose, an airplane coming home and landing. The trees provided a peaceful background. In this picture, fire lights the way instead of destroying the whole scene. It seemed Bob was starting to learn to use his own energy to find a pathway for himself, and that he was using his aggressive energy constructively at last. It was also interesting that Bob had now chosen five matches after using only four matches in the volcano picture. He seemed increasingly more confident of his ability to control and use this element properly.

The airplane also suggests the sky motif, a fourth element after water, fire and land. The airplane could take off and land freely, but in Bob's own life, with its many ups and downs, there was no clear pathway to the sky. However, I did feel he was moving forward and that he had a "landing strip," that is to say a base to work from. His destructive fire had now become light, and his well-rooted earth and trees seemed to show stability.

The palm tree probably symbolizes the more exotic, intuitive side of his nature, and the more common oak tree stands for his life in the community and in his home. Both were becoming more firmly established at this time. Before I left town, I asked Bob's teachers for a report on his progress. They said he was doing much better in his schoolwork and showing a real sense of responsibility.

During our work together, Bob and I did not have to analyze his symbols. I often simply developed a feeling for what the picture meant. I believe that too much analysis stifles the naturally-occuring healing process. I did, however, sometimes ask Bob what a certain figure meant to him so that I could better understand what was happening inside him. But it was not only the meaning of his symbols that was ultimately important; it was also the healing process itself that concerned us—and later, how it was manifested in his collective world of home and school.

In the course of his sandplay therapy, Bob began to reunite with parts of himself that had been wounded or cut off. At the beginning of his treatment he would not even talk to me, much less communicate his pains and fears. By the end of our time together, Bob and I were friends. This change in our relationship came about mainly because we had stuck together through all the stages and spirals of his development. Most certainly this boy's journey went from the watery flooding stage (vegetative) to the second stage, and finally to the third or adaptation-to-the-collective stage.

The watery or vegetative stage lasted for much longer with Bob than it does with most children. In fact some of his fighting scenes took place on precarious bridges and over what looked like dangerous waters; some of these scenes involved fighting with fire, which was eventually contained within the circle. His last (adaptive) stage displayed more of the play element than in most children, though for Bob this seemed essential and quite right. He had fought so aggressively since his kindergarten days that playing proved very joyful for him. A new dimension — humor — seemed to awaken in him.

Bob's therapy was different from that of any other child I have worked with; yet his path followed the hero's journey in its own individual way. It seemed that after acting out all his required stages in the sandtray, Bob was ready for a more peaceful life at home and at school. Certainly he was happier, more centered and thinking in his actions. Without experiencing the positive and negative symbols that he expressed so clearly in his sandtray pictures, I feel he would not have found his way.

6

ENRICHMENT THROUGH SYMBOLS

It is not easy for me to write about Joe because he and his family have become very close to me. And Joe's imaginative world, which he expressed in the sandtray, is so rich and unusual that it is difficult to describe.

Joe was seven when he first came to see me. From his first visit I had a sense of his remarkable and creative personality. Joe was a lively and basically happy child, but he had serious problems with his family and peers. His schoolwork also presented problems. His recently divorced parents exhibited a good deal of hostility towards each other. Joe's father was ill at ease and unable to play with his son. Joe's mother was an alcoholic full of anger and hurt about life in general. She really cared about Joe, however, and wanted to be the best of mothers for him. Sometimes, however, she could not cope with her own frustrations and seemed unable to stop venting her unhappiness and anger on the boy and others close to her.

From the beginning, Joe seemed comfortable making scenes in the sandtray. Even his very first picture was quite complicated and full of symbolic meanings (Figure 17). He began the scene by placing eight houses and four trees in a crescent shape. The arc started on the west side of the box with a log cabin, and ended on the east side with a castle. Joe often used this castle in later pictures. Behind a red-roofed house, in the center of the crescent, Joe built a pen and fenced in some sheep. He placed some deer and rabbits outside the sheep pen, explaining that these animals were free.

On the southeast side of the box, Joe made a stream and placed a boat on it, then he built a bridge over the stream, near which in turn he put three turtles and a Chinese house. To the right of the turtles, Joe placed the figures of ten people and told me they were attending a lecture. This explanation struck me, for it showed that from the beginning of his treatment Joe knew that one can learn from the quiet and spiritual side of life. It was interesting to me that he seemed to realize that a Chinese house or shrine near a stream could be another part of a meaningful picture.

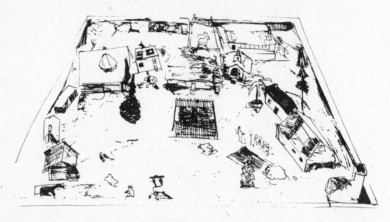

FIGURE 17

Joe then put figures of people on the porches of houses. In the center of the sandtray were many boxes of supplies. He put a square fence around some trees near the supplies, and told me that this was a special religious shrine. Apparently Joe realized that the shrine was just as important a form of nourishment as the boxes of food. The last thing Joe did was put a Chinese bridge, a shrine, and three trees in the south center. "This is a kind of old town with plenty of supplies," he said, again seeming to realize that spiritual beliefs and feelings would be an important part of the supplies of an old town. Then he lowered his voice to a near whisper and said, "There was so much to choose from. I do like you."

Joe was delighted with the new world of the sandtray. Playing in the sand gave him the freedom to talk to me about some of his problems at school. He said the boys ganged up on him. He also began to talk about his home and about his many frightening nightmares.

Joe's next two pictures were on the same theme of wordly and spiritual security. He called his second picture a safe island for all the animals. Again he placed food supplies on the island, and chose the same Chinese bridge and shrine to stand near the supplies.

Joe's third picture also contained the Chinese bridge and shrine. This picture, however, was not all about safety—it also depicted a train stuck in a snow storm. I was soon to learn that when Joe made snow storms in the sand, things were going badly for him at home or at school. These snow storms seemed to release Joe's energy and help him understand feelings of frustration and anger which he otherwise had trouble expressing.

Joe called his next scene a desert. First he told me men were fighting in it, then he changed his mind and said, "No, it's a parade. I really don't like wars." The desert was a very important symbol for Joe; I later realized that through desert scenes Joe was in part expressing his own sense of emotional suffocation.

Joe made many snow storms during this period. In one, he placed the American flag in the center of the storm. By doing so, Joe was probably expressing his strong sense of identity and belonging, despite the suffocation and cold anger around him. I felt from the start that Joe was strong enough to withstand the storms in his life fairly well. In another snow scene, Joe built his picture around a creche depicting the birth of Jesus, explaining that Jesus was born in the winter. This scene, filled with many beautiful and life-giving symbols, included a ming tree, with a large owl and a robin in its branches near the creche. In the center of the picture was a small lake with a penguin near its bank. Joe seemed to realize that even with his anger and frustration he was in touch with some center of inner peace and harmony.

I wondered, at the time, about how Joe was able to work through so much of his anger in these snow scenes. But later I realized that nature and natural events—such as snow storms—can be very logical and obvious symbols for Joe's emotions and frustrations and their effects upon his interior landscape.

Joe's capacity to love was either being met with the indifference of his father's excessive logic or overwhelmed by his mother's frustrations, demands and anger. Combined with his school problems, these parental problems doubled Joe's burden. In his desire to love his parents and peers and be helpful to them, Joe was either being frozen out, as he showed in his snow scenes, or burnt up, as he depicted in his desert scenes. He started his work with me feeling that his capacity to love was stuck somewhere between burning and freezing. The freezing snow storms and scorching desert scenes helped Joe free his emotions and begin to understand them.

Joe next made a lovely picture of several houses standing near a lake (Figure 18). He placed some turtles and a mouse near the lake, and a swan and some ducks in the lake. Typically, Joe combined practicality and beauty, putting a water pump in the lake with pipes leading up to the houses. He also built a bridge over the lake, explaining that it was "for boats to go under." He put seven dwarves as workers near the houses, again mingling fantasy with everyday practicality. The last thing Joe did was put a white horse and a black one close together in the sand. He said the horses were very good friends, and the picture shows them in a very loving relationship to each other. This scene was strong and constructive, and it showed me that Joe was growing and changing. In fact, I was getting reports from his school that his academic work was improving. His teachers were beginning to appreciate Joe's creativity, but he was still having problems relating to his peers, especially the boys.

FIGURE 18

At his next session, Joe made another desert scene but then changed it to a snow scene. As he did so he asked, "Can there be a storm in the desert? Are there bears in a desert?" I was as puzzled by his desert snow storm as he was, but I suggested that perhaps the cold winds bearing snow had come down to the desert from Canada or Alaska. Joe looked at me for a minute, then said, "I wish we'd go to Alaska so my mother could cool off her temper." I asked him if he could tell his mother something about this, and he quickly replied, "Oh no! That would not be good. It just came from my head to you."

On his next visit, Joe made a scene of destruction, saying that a volcano had come up out of the ocean and destroyed the land. He kept trying to figure out how he could depict the sand blowing up. Then Joe asked me how long I had had the miniatures and the sandtray. When I answered "About eight years," he said, "But that is how long you have been separated from me!" He had just celebrated his eighth birthday, and it was like him to make this kind of statement, very analytic, very abstract and very loving.

The following week was a bad one for Joe's family. His mother became very angry and so upset that she kicked Joe out of the house, according to his father, who telephoned to make arrangements to bring Joe over to my office. Joe immediately started playing war games with the miniature dinosaurs, buildings and boats (Figure 19). He had the dinosaurs attacking the buildings and boats, then each other. Then he told me the following story about his war:

FIGURE 19

"Once there was a little town and one day a man came back. He said he had been to a native village. The villagers had a volcano god that brought back dinosaurs to terrorize the world because the it was angry that the villagers had destroyed all of the jungles and forests. The volcano blew up and let the dinosaurs out of its cork. The hot lava wrecked the houses but the dinosaurs could stand it even though it was so hot.

"The villagers fled from the town and a few of the trucks are filled with some pterodactyls. The volcano found an underground opening and finally blew itself to pieces. Finally, the dinosaurs started fighting each other and one killed the other for food. One man was in his bathroom and did not know about the fighting. A dinosaur wrecked his tub, and he was so scared that he came out running two hundred miles a minute in his bathrobe. There was a big whirlpool that caught a dactyl and he was drowned, but before he was killed a big log went through his right wing. There was a Chinese house and a bridge floating around because it lost its foundation. A saber-tooth cat was climbing up on a tree. He fell back into the hot lava and that was the end of him. There was a big Indian canoe wreck and a big rock crashed into a castle wall. There was a boat with a ladder and a man climbed on it into the castle tower. A dinosaur accidentally stepped on a submarine and it blew up and made the town go up in smoke from all the fires. One rock blew up in the explosion and all that was left was a big hole in the middle or bottom of the rock. Three trees survived through all of this—a willow, a pine, and an old oak tree."

Where did this vivid and striking story come from? It was certainly quite an accomplished and coherent fantasy for an eight-year-old boy to make up. At first it seemed as if parts of it were the synopsis of a television monster movie. Despite its amusing and entertaining elements, I knew that it was a serious and important story for Joe. The only story he ever told me in detail, it seemed to flow just effortlessly. He told the story so quickly that I had difficulty writing it down. I was moved by it and tried to evaluate and understand its symbolism, but it was too complex for me to be really sure of its meaning. I feel sure that the exploding rock stood for Joe's fear of his mother's anger at the time.

Joe's understanding of trees amazed me. There was always a kind of old-world connection to nature and myth in Joe's psyche. I was quite moved that he knew the trees would survive. I think that the oak tree, abundant in his neighborhood and at his school, symbolized community life for Joe, on which he placed lasting value. Pine trees are very hardy, live for centuries, and are evergreens. They also live in wild regions too arid and desolate for other trees. Joe thus seemed to choose the pine tree to stand for both the free and the wild, and the life-sustaining qualities of nature. The willow cannot live on barren slopes; it needs water and a secret, shaded place. It has often been associated with secrets and mysteries. Joe seemed to realize that the willow has a magical significance, especially when he used it near his shrines in the sandtray; he would speak of it in connection with certain fairy tales. He often put the willow near the Chinese shrine and bridge, speaking of it in terms of what he understood of Oriental life.

The willow, the pine and the oak tree all survived the story's general destruction. Somehow Joe realized that the human community, the beauty and sustenance of nature, and the understanding and wisdom that come from spiritual awareness, are values which would survive the most violent and angry eruptions.

Joe made his sand picture with the dinosaurs and trees before telling his story. As I looked at the scene I wondered about how such a seemingly calm and simple arrangement could have been the basis for such a rich and violent fantasy. Yet Joe's story and actions showed that the destruction was very real to him. In the story and sand picture, Joe expressed and faced his own fear and anger at his mother's seemingly violent behavior. Facing these frightening emotions, he seemed ready to change or enlarge his ego and psyche by being more in touch with a strong and positive self. And it seemed to make him aware that he could and would survive his present ordeal.

One very important day, Joe made a zoo scene with a well organized series of cages. A father was feeding the animals. He had a hoe with him to protect himself from the bears, Joe told me. The father was near a pond. A pelican in the pond was biting an elephant's tail, telling him to stay out of her pond. At this time Joe's father was finally becoming relaxed enough with his son to play with him at times. Their improving relationship seemed to be reflected in this happy and playful scene.

Joe combined all three stages—stasis, struggle, and adaptation—in his treatment, and even expressed them concurrently. He always seemed to have a connection with the quiet vegetative phase, as his understanding of trees and their significance would show. He also knew about the quiet beauty of water, and used it to represent calm and harmony in his sand scenes. He also seemed to be in touch with animals, to have a real psychic connection with the turtle and mouse—both symbols of earth and endurance, much like the trees which he said would survive.

Joe made other scenes of destruction, but not as fiery ones as other boys usually do. I felt that Joe probably lived too close to the fires of erupting emotions in his family to need to use destructive fires in his sandtrays. Although he often used candles and lanterns, these were mostly used for their light alone. He did, however, need to destroy his connection with old adaptive ways of behavior and old, painful feelings, as he showed when he made his volcano picture and told his story.

Joe made several other fighting and struggle scenes. In one, soldiers are protecting the castle in the north center of the tray. To the right, on the eastern side of the tray, is a red catapult and an army tank. In the center, all the way across the tray, he made a landing field and showed one airplane coming in to land. The landing field, a sort of identity symbol and earth space for many boys, seems to be a good sign that one is finding both one's true path and the stable values one can return to. I felt that the landing field had this sort of meaning for Joe as well.

At the south end of the tray, Joe dug out a large lake and placed five boats in it. Army equipment and trucks protect the lake's western shore. Last, Joe placed four trees and two houses on a hill in the southwest corner. This struggle scene, like all of Joe's war scenes, had more to do with protection and security than it did with violence. There was often room in his war scenes for houses, trees and lakes.

Joe was now learning how to get in touch with his anger. One day his mother came with him to therapy and made a sarcastic remark about one of his sand pictures. Joe immediately demolished the scene, which had already been photographed. I was glad to see him react so quickly and express his anger so effectively. He told me that although he still did not like to fight with the boys at school, he could now defend himself when necessary. His teacher confirmed this when she discussed his progress at school with me. Joe was learning to accept the fact that he liked to play with girls at times and related well with them. Girls, he explained, are more creative and like to make things. I knew the boys often teased Joe for playing with the girls, but I was glad to see that he could now accept this part of himself and stand up for his right to do things he liked to do. He was amazingly creative, and it was easy for me to see why he preferred making things to fighting. I have never known a child who could use sticks, paper, string, or any other scraps so creatively.

At this time, Joe made several pictures of animals visiting each other in their homes. He made a very interesting house for a mouse, built of cardboard, with a little shovel placed outside to keep snow from the doorway. He made a picture using the miniature Noah's ark, with all the animals parading up the gangplank in pairs. Interestingly, he added angels. In one of his mouse scenes with the cardboard house, he placed a little girl feeding chickens outside. This figure seemed to symbolize Joe's own position in life at this time: he was beginning to be able to stand outside the houses of both of his parents, to be strong enough to be able to separate himself from their wishes and demands. And he was becoming strong enough to recognize and use the feminine and creative aspects of his nature, and to realize that the development of his inner psyche was instrumental in giving him the strength to stand on his own outside of each house.

Joe made seven fantasy scenes using the figures of the seven dwarves. One of them seemed to give a very clear picture of the inner and outer journey Joe was making at this time (Figure 20).

He dug a wide stream at the northern end of the tray and had the seven dwarves crossing the stream on a long, narrow bridge. The bridge and the stream, which were the focal point of the picture, formed a long cross. This seemed to be significant, and may or may not have related to Joe's strong Jewish background. He seemed to be carrying a heavy cross in his own life, and perhaps the figure of the cross had a deep significance for him. Like many of his other scenes, this one had elements which carried a spiritual significance, such as the willow and ming trees, the Chinese shrine, and perhaps even the fish and owls.

FIGURE 20

On the east or right side of this picture is the stream. In the water are three whales, as well as a fish, a duck, and a sea horse. The seven dwarves are crossing the the river on a bridge, and the first dwarf is carrying a light. On the bank of the river behind the dwarves is a big ming tree, with a large bird nesting in its branches. A Chinese tiger is crouching near the roots of the tree. Close by are several other small animals, including the owl, which always had a special significance for Joe. The owl often represents the mystery of night and the beauty and dark poetry of life.

Two smaller trees are placed on either side of the ming tree. Across the river, on the west side of the tray, Snow White is standing outside the house of the dwarves, waiting for them to return. Near the house are two trees and two mice. A bird and a rabbit are also playing close to the house, and Joe has not forgotten to include his Chinese bridge on the western bank of the river. All Joe's pictures are so intricately made and so rich in detail that it is difficult to describe them accurately. This picture is no exception.

Obviously, the dwarves are coming home from the workaday world to their fantasy-house across the water. Perhaps Joe himself identifies with the dwarf carrying the light; he put light in most of his pictures and seemed to really understand the need for some sort of awareness to light the way.

The orderliness and symmetry of this picture are both striking. The two smaller trees frame the ming tree perfectly. On both banks of the river, trees, animals, and people all seem to be in their proper places. The strange Chinese tiger under the ming tree may be guarding this world of fantasy and expressing a warning to keep alert, and not lose touch with owls and other creatures of the night.

Joe was doing very well in school by now. He also seemed to be taking his home life in stride. Joe was away with his father for a few weeks, and when he came back he made a snow scene again, telling me that the cows' teats were frozen; he left, however, many food supplies for the people. He then made a beautiful sand candle and told me that he had not forgotten the importance of light. He shared more of his monster dreams with me.

Then Joe made a beach scene for me, because he knew I was going away on a holiday soon. Summer vacation was approaching, and he was going away as well. This beach scene was a picture of another secret place, he explained. Across the water on a far distant shore stood a willow tree and a palm tree. Only a sailboat could take people there, Joe said.

In the fall, Joe changed schools for several good reasons. The change worked out well and Joe was happy at his new school. He shared many of his experiences there with me, saying I was still his best friend. I was glad to see that he had made friends of his own age at the new school. At this point Joe made many more dwarf scenes and some beautiful pieces out of clay. One of these he called "a little boy's hike up the steep mountain," and it really was all about a journey up a spiral road to a mountain top. Joe also made a mountain out of clay, with a road spiraling up its sides. On the top of the mountain he placed the tiny figure of a little boy. Joe was certainly aware of the mountain, the path, and the journey. He wanted me to keep this lovely model.

Another school year and another year of therapy seemed to slip by quickly. Joe was growing both physically and emotionally. The following fall, he felt ready to go back to his own school in his own neighborhood. He had many friends now and happily adjusted to the school which had been an unhappy place for him earlier. Although I felt that Joe no longer needed serious therapy, his parents asked me to see him occasionally, as many problems had yet to be ironed out between them, which they felt might be affecting Joe. The mother in particular needed my support; she was getting professional help for herself now, and seemed to be facing her own problems more adequately.

During his visits with me, Joe continued to make creative sand pictures. One was a very realistic scene of the big dam in Colorado. Another was filled with symbols meaningful to Joe. He made a circular island within a moat, then placed his favorite castle on it. He put moss around the castle and said that the place was old and not known by many people. The horses knew of it, however, and they came to the island to eat and drink. Joe chose a blue and a red horse, both from a collection of Chinese magic horses, and placed them on the island near the castle. A third Chinese horse, a white one, was watching from the bank. Blue and red together seemed to signify passion and spirit united. The white horse on the book balanced the group and seemed to be looking over or checking out the entire scene. To place the white horse where Joe did seemed right, especially since white is often a symbol for the intellect. Joe seemed to be more in touch with all his fantasy life now. He still had some monster dreams which he shared with me, but they did not paralyze him with fright as his earlier dreams did. He could laugh about some of these monster dreams now, and seemed to understand that they sometimes came from a part of his own psyche.

Joe still comes to see me occasionally. He is now nine and a half years old. One recent sand picture of his is very lovely. As he finished it, he simply said, "That is really full of life, isn't it?" I had to agree that it was. The picture was very detailed; Joe had even made a sort of temple out of corrugated cardboard to cover the Buddha. He placed this temple on the right side of the picture, appropriately enough on the eastern side, with a tree, a light, and a treasure house in front of it. A long river spirals down from the northwest corner of the sandtray, ending its journey at the southeast corner. At the head of the river Joe placed the white Chinese madonna, Kwan-yin. In the river he put some ducks, some fish and a swan. A large frog nearly blocks the river at its southeast end, and there is another frog in the river nearer the top of the watercourse. Joe again chose the blue and the red Chinese horses, and placed them together in a protected place at the northeast corner. A workhorse and some ducks stand in the center. Again, at the extreme northern end of the picture the white horse stands alone and watches the scene. Across the river towards the center of the tray are a baboon mother and baby, a peacock, and the willow tree which Joe so often used in his scenes. Near the tree are a Chinese boy and girl. There are many small animals, rabbits, bear cubs, and a mouse. To the west is a wise old owl in a tree, watching the young animals as they play.

Many other creative and happy pictures have been part of Joe's more recent visits with me. On a rather thoughtful kind of day, he made another picture using the castle. He placed it and two trees in the north center of the picture, and made an intricate road leading up to the castle. There are some cars and trucks on the road, near which he put a little hollowed-out wooden shelter that he had often used to cover and protect the smaller animals. The last thing Joe did was place a white rock—which he had used in several previous sand pictures—near the bottom or southern end of the road. When I asked about the rock, he explained that "It's my favorite sitting place." He showed me once more how in touch with life he was. This picture was unusual for many reasons, an important one being that the magical castle was now accessible to some, and not in such a secret hidden place as before.

The last two pictures I have described, along with all of Joe's other pictures, make a very complex and intricate use of symbols. Here I will try to amplify the meaning of some of the many symbols Joe used—miniatures of trees, owls, bears, dwarves and other working people, the peacock, the Chinese shrine and bridge, horses, the castle, the mouse, and the white stone. All these symbols were important to Joe and each had its share in enriching his life.

Joe's own long story, in which the willow, oak and pine trees survive an otherwise general destruction, explains better than I can his knowledge of the eternal, life-oriented symbolism of trees. Dwarves are both part of the working world and part of Joe's fantasy world. They need light and human understanding to pass freely between these worlds. The bear and the owl are both animals which relate to the mother. The owl certainly stands for the instinctive portion of Joe's awareness. The bear, both loving and ferocious, was closely tied to Joe's feelings about all the women in his life, but especially his mother and teachers who could change moods suddenly and seemingly without warning. The peacock has many meanings. For Joe, I feel two are important. We talked mostly about the many eyes which a peacock has in its colored feathers and about the beautiful colors of these feathers. The peacock seems to mean both beauty and an all-inclusive kind of wisdom to Joe.

The mouse is very close to the earth, a humble little animal and a favorite of Joe's. He once brought me a white miniature mouse to go with my dark one, then built a small house for the mice to live in. No doubt Joe identified with the smallness of the mice and with their self-sufficiency against great odds.

All the Chinese symbols Joe used obviously had a religious significance for him, perhaps because his Judaism came out of the Mideast and shares common ground with some elements of Oriental mysticism. One of Joe's grandfathers was very interested in Oriental art and design. This grandfather designed Oriental interiors for houses and Oriental gardens.

The castle is another spiritual symbol. It seemed to be a secret and safe place for Joe. He seemed to make castle scenes on his quiet and thoughtful days, as if he needed a peaceful place to sit and think. The white rock which Joe placed outside the castle in many of his pictures was a really self-defining symbol for Joe. He seemed to see himself sitting and thinking on the rock outside the castle. The rock itself has much inner symbolism of eternity and peace. This particular stone is well shaped and is not often used by other children who come to see me, although adults often use it in their sand pictures. When Joe said the rock was his "sitting place," I needed no further explanation of the stone's meaning for Joe.

When Joe comes to see me now, sometimes we talk, sometimes he makes a sand picture. Occasionally we just meet as friends. I was glad when he told me one day, "Too much time with adults makes me nervous. I really like to play with my friends." He made one remark I will never forget. I was talking with his father and we were making some too general remarks about people and life. Suddenly I realized what I was doing and asked, "How can we adults judge people like this?"

Joe very quickly responded: "It's like I can sit in this chair and be me, but if other people did not know me they could see me in all kinds of ways. I guess I really like myself because I feel good inside." Obviously he likes other people too. It was wonderful to me to realize that Joe was so deeply sure of himself and others, an attitude unusual in an adult, and certainly a real accomplishment in one less than ten years old. At this point, Joe certainly does not seem to need further therapy. I feel that he is so in touch with himself that he really is living out his own richly symbolic life, his own inner myth, every day. I hope his life will continue moving in this richly creative way, not denying the many daily frustrations and problems he may face, but dealing with them in a conscious way.

7

A HEROES JOURNEY

Once upon a time long ago, a young boy named Jack sat by the seashore and drew pictures in the sand. All the people came to laugh at him, not only because he drew pictures, but because they could see that he was only half a boy. The could see Jack did not know how to do anything but draw pictures, that he could not find the part of himself that would grow and become a man who did other things besides draw pictures on the beach and daydream.

Although they laughed at him, the people realized the boy was very good at drawing pictures. They saw that his drawings were both beautiful and important. Jack's pictures were mostly of horses and bears. One day he drew a horse that was both real and dreamlike. It was so beautiful that when the King heard about it he came to see it. The King was so caught and charmed by the dream represented in the drawing that he said to the boy, "Jack, you must take a journey and find the horse that will redeem our kingdom."

But Jack did not want to leave the seashore, even at the King's command. He did not want to leave his pictures and dreams. By now he was used to all the teasing, which gave him an identity and a place on the beach. The people eventually grew tired of trying to disturb his drawings and were content to jeer at him from a distance, calling him a half-wit. Jack had come to accept the role of a scapegoat. Happy in his world, he filled his life with fantasy.

But he knew he could not disobey the King's command. The King had said, "You must be tested, diagnosed, and observed. You must not just sit by the seashore and draw pictures in the sand. Really, boy, you must leave our village. You must be forged in the fire, and above all you must find the Real Horse, a beautiful dream and a real dream, and bring him back to us."

So, in sadness, the boy left the beach and set off to find the horse of his picture. He whistled to keep up his spirits, because the outside world was dark and frightening. Jack was so frightened he was almost ready to lie down and give up the search when a strange thing happened. Suddenly, an odd looking bear appeared and stood in front of Jack on the road. This bear's face looked almost human and it could talk. The bear told Jack to follow him down a path that would not be easy. No matter how difficult it might be, the bear said they should follow the path together. Only in this way would Jack find the rest of himself, the doing and becoming part which would make him a whole boy, and later, a whole man. Once this happened he would be able to continue his journey and find the remarkable horse to take back to his own kingdom. The bear then described the fires Jack would find at the end of the path, fires he would have to go through in order to become a whole man.

Jack listened to the bear and followed him. He stuck to the path, no matter how hard it was. Just as the bear predicted, Jack went through the fires at the end of the path and did find the rest of himself. But Jack's journey did not end with the fires. He had to keep on going until he came to the house of an old woman who held the dream horse prisoner in her pasture. Now that he had gone through the fires and was whole, Jack knew both how to recognize his dream and how to fight to obtain the horse.

Besides the horse, the old woman also held a beautiful princess captive. Jack recognized the princess as part of his dream and his journey, and realized that she also had to be freed from the old woman's tyranny. So Jack fought long and hard, rescued the princess and the horse, and took them both back to the King who had need of such living and powerful dreams.

This myth comes from an old Malayan tale. I have changed the story slightly to tell the real story of a thirteen-year-old boy who was one of the first children to use sandplay with me. It tells of our hard work together. For Jack, sandplay therapy was the fiery path which helped him find his whole self by connecting his world of dreams with the learning and growing part of himself so that healing could take place.

Jack had been to many doctors and therapists before he came to see me with a file thicker than any I had seen before; a folder full of questions with no answers, diagnoses and problems with no solutions. He had had every possible type of medical and psychometric examination, and many psychiatric evaluations.

School had always been full of problems for Jack, and obviously a nightmare to him. He did not really attend to his schoolwork because he spent most of his energy running away from his schoolmates. He was really deathly afraid of his peers, who made him their scapegoat when they saw he was in a world of his own. Jack's schoolmates interpreted his dreaminess for weakness, and made him the object of jeers and physical attacks. Although Jack was physically well-built, he was small for his age. His face, filled with insecurity and fear, rather than his actual physical size, made him a target. Because Jack kept running away from school, his principal had recommended me to his parents. Jack could not be stopped from running away, and neither the school authorities nor Jack's parents, who were desperately concerned, knew what to do to help the boy.

I read Jack's file to learn about his background. Both of his parents were professionals. Jack was the youngest child in the family. One brother was still in high school while another had graduated from college and was living away from home. Although Jack had tested as having above-average intelligence, he was doing poorly in every subject, and actually failing arithmetic. Nothing in the files helped explain the reasons for his failure in all of his subjects at school. Nor did any explain why he was so miserable.

Because he did not know how to deal with a world which seemed hostile and truly terrifying to him, Jack would escape into his fantasy world. This was the only answer to the question of why he had no interest in school. He could not always sit still long enough to pay attention to his lessons. Only by escaping could Jack let out some of the inner anger brought on by the teasing and bullying of his peers. Whenever he could, Jack would pretend to be ill so he could go home. Otherwise, he would just walk away from school. Jack had dealt with the teasing in every way except the powerful and helpful way of standing up for himself and actually facing his tormentors.

Jack's world of fantasy and daydreams was his greatest defense against the painful situation at school. In class he would refuse to answer questions, probably because he did not even hear them. Most of his teachers let him daydream since he caused no real problems for them; he would sit quietly, think his own thoughts and draw his beautiful pictures. A few teachers had tried, more or less unsuccessfully, to reach him individually. But most had given up by the time Jack came to see me. His reputation was such that little academic work was expected of him. He was allowed to spend most of his time in school drawing very creative pictures of his fantasies and then destroying them immediately, or hiding them.

Just as the boy in the Malayan myth spent all of his days at the seashore, dreaming and drawing his dream-pictures, so Jack did nothing but fantasize, draw, and hide from others. In Jack's case, the principal and the parents commanded him to leave his fantasy world, just as the King did in the myth. They said to me, "As a therapist, you must find a way for this boy to make his journey. You will give him help to mend his split personality. You will redirect his energy." They gave the commands, yet they themselves did not sound very hopeful. They had been waiting for Jack to begin his journey for a long time.

When he first came to see me, he brought pictures of saber-toothed cats and a picture of a real-looking rattlesnake squeezing a baby snake coiled inside a larger snake (Figure 21). He traced his own left hand and showed where the snake's fangs had bit him. Realistic blood drips down the hand.

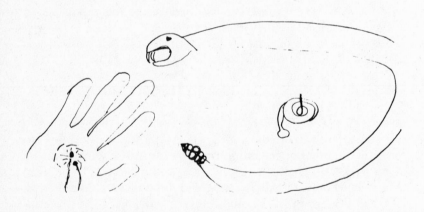

FIGURE 21

Jack also drew some new pictures on his first visits with me. He drew a bomb hidden inside of his school locker. "To blow up the school," he said. He drew a picture of himself, then changed it to a soldier holding many guns and shooting them all at his peers, whom he named. All the pictures were violent and rather frightening to look at. The picture of the evil-looking snake drawing blood from Jack's left hand was, for me, more realistic and perhaps symbolic than the rest of his drawings. In looking at this picture, I certainly got the message that I had a boy in real need of help; I also knew our work together would be difficult and perhaps take much time.

My first sessions with Jack were tense, because he was full of hostility, anger, and frustration. Sometimes I felt the whole room would explode with the intensity of his feelings, but he could express very few of them verbally. However, he did share his very realistic drawings with me, and make sand pictures. Jack's first sand picture was rather peaceful, just as he himself seemed peaceful and calm outside (Figure 22A). In it, Jack was showing me the face he presented to the world, his exterior self. He called this picture a desert scene, and showed fighting going on. Yet the fighting was of a secretive

FIGURE 22A

and hidden kind, as most of the soldiers and equipment were camouflaged and half-buried in the sand. Jack put a stream down the center of the box, and said that the soldiers were fighting over the water. Jack was indicating quite clearly that he was choked off from his own emotions. He had to fight to find his way through the desert and regain the water which he had lost. I was not surprised when he told me that he liked going to the desert with his family. The desert was in harmony with his own calm and desolate exterior self. When he went to the desert with his family, Jack collected rocks. One of his favorite activities, this was the only thing he truly enjoyed doing with his family. The rocks were very important symbols to Jack. More than part of the calm and desolate desert, rocks were part of a hidden beauty which he could own and keep secretly for himself. Ugly and drab on the outside, rocks often hide beautiful and valuable treasures on the inside, if they are split open and polished. As I got to know Jack better, I came to understand why rocks were an abiding symbol for him. Certainly, he himself was hiding much emotional beauty inside, where others could not see.

After this first picture, Jack's emotions seemed to explode in many ways. He made many scenes of war and destruction the likes of which, for frightening realism and intensity, I have not since seen any child create and act out. Jack would take up the figures of soldiers and ask to cut off their heads. If I suggested he not do this, he would take red crayon and cover the figures in blood. He could sustain very real and bloodcurdling war noises for a half hour or more at a time.

Making these battle scenes in the sandtray seemed to prepare Jack to express his own hostile feelings and the aggressions of other people in his life. He told me his brother in high school was very mean to him, putting him down verbally and incessantly teasing him. He said he always spilled everything, and that his family was disgusted with him all the time.

After this talk about his family, Jack made a lovely clay model. With the utmost care and patience, he modeled his entire family seated at the dinner table. He fashioned chairs, a table, and a chandelier out of the clay. Just as I had finished admiring this delicate and creative piece, Jack reached up as high as he could with his hand and smashed the entire piece on the floor. Just before he smashed it, he hesitated, his hand poised in mid-air, and asked: "Can I smash this?" I had to reply, "Yes, if you must." I believe Jack was as startled as I was when his work broke into hundreds of pieces. And he was very surprised I did not "yell at him," as he expressed it. I did, however, let him know I was disappointed with the loss of such of a beautiful piece of work.

Now it was time to pick up the pieces, and Jack and I did it together. Why did he destroy this lovely model? I felt he had destroyed the clay piece in anger and frustration because he realized his family was not like the clay model, eating together in real harmony and peace. Whatever the reason, it seemed to be a good release for Jack. He did not seem as hostile or inwardly angry after this.

Jack continued to make battle scenes in the sand and to actively participate in the wars he depicted. He also drew pictures of time machines going back and forth in time. These pictures said something to me about his own development and regression.

Most of Jack's battles seemed to be between Arabs and Americans, like his first scene, fought in the desert over some kind of water supply. Describing these battles, he used quite colorful language. He once ordered one of the soldiers: "Get up, you fool, and fight!" He explained this was a gruesome battle going on and that the soldier was a coward. For a long time Jack insisted on destroying and burying all of the equipment and soldiers in his pictures, so I could not take pictures of many of them.

Later on, however, his battles became more organized and less violent. He began to be concerned with building and destroying, bringing in construction equipment, and letting his pictures stand when they were completed. He also began to use water more freely, making scenes of the sea. In one battle, he said that the boats hit some rocks in the ocean and sank. His waves in this picture were very realistic (Figure 22B). I felt it was a good sign when Jack began to use water in his battle scenes. It showed he was getting in touch with his emotions and was less fearful of opening himself to them than he had been earlier.

FIGURE 22B

Jack was now completing his first year of treatment with me. His teachers, very surprised at the changes in Jack's behavior, began sending good reports about him. He began to participate in class and no longer daydreamed and kept to himself as much. He even made a few friends. Jack did not come to see me during the summer, but he did phone me a few times to let me know how he was doing.

Jack returned in the fall for more work. His first sand picture was called "The Battle of Hell in the Black Desert." He commented on this violent battle scene: "No one wins; all the tanks are destroyed; I feel the war was terrible. I don't think I want to do any more war scenes. Too many men were lost and the battle was too expensive, with all of the equipment lost and destroyed." At the end of the hour, he added: "I guess my feeling about the war (the Vietnam War was still going on) is that it is bad."

I had several conferences with Jack's parents during his time in therapy with me. Finally they told me that Jack's life was going well, both at home and at school. He was relating well to his schoolmates, and even felt free enough with them to help plan and carry out some mischievous pranks. Except for arithmetic, his academic work had improved greatly and he was now considered average.

Jack made several more sand pictures. He made scenes of mines, and many of the desert. Unlike his earlier battle pictures with soldiers manning tanks and guns, these later ones were filled with working people doing construction work and mining. He made one in the shape of a lovely spiral of trucks and equipment. The spiral is in the shape of an "S", drawn backwards. It starts with four work trucks on the west side of the tray, and moves all the way around to the east corner, with seven pieces of army equipment comprising the middle and end of the spiral. Inside the western part of the "S" curve are trucks hauling minerals and coal out of a mine shaft. In all these mining scenes, Jack seemed to restate his own interest in rocks and their hidden beauty.

Jack said the army equipment on the right or east side of the spiral was to protect the mine from Arabs who were trying to steal the minerals. The Arabs and their camels circle inside of the top part of the spiral.

This picture is certainly about the theme of the journey, depicted in a very masculine way, the trucks and army equipment standing for strength and motion. Yet the gentle shape of the spiral seems to symbolize a path which will move through fighting towards harmony and peace.

Jack, like the boy in the Malayan myth, had to go out into the world to fight his battles and find the part of himself which would make him a whole person. This is very much the masculine way. It seemed to me, at this point, that Jack, like the boy in the myth, was winning his battle with the old witch and gaining, by this victory, the energy to separate himself from his fantasies in order to understand them and reunite them with his more conscious individual and social self. For Jack, the friendly bear who showed the path and gave help and encouragement was probably the therapist. With my trust and help, Jack stopped fearing and being fascinated by the frightening and blood-sucking snake which had been so much a part of his early fantasy life. Perhaps this dangerous fantasy animal was a part of his healing process as well. In the end, Jack did become a whole and a happy person. Many of the questions of how and why this happened will probably never be answered; rational answers such as these do not always matter.

Now, ten years after beginning his treatment with me, Jack is twenty-four years old. He is a strong, healthy and fine-looking man. He finished high school and took two years of junior college, then chose to work with his father on their horse and cattle ranch, which he now quite capably manages. I hear from Jack each Christmas and sometimes during the year. Jack is very important to me, partly because he was one of the first children who used sandtray therapy with me, but mostly because he is most surely living out his own myth. He began as a unique and sensitive child who struggled and fought his way bravely toward healing. Jack introduced me to the mysterious deep process of healing which takes place with the aid of the sandtray and a sheltered place. This process continues to be just as mysteriously renewing and beautiful for me as it was when Jack and I first met and he started on his journey to wholeness and found his other half in the process.

The Feminine Way

8

INTEGRATION OF INSTINCTS

The young girl whose story I will tell in this chapter followed a very beautiful and individual path to healing. I will try to show how Sarah's development is similar to that of other girls and different from that of boys. More importantly, I will show how she follows her own natural and sure-footed way, revealing her own distinct nature in the healing process.

Although Sarah was ten years old when she first came to me, she acted like a much younger child. A look at Sarah's family dynamics gave me some idea of the reason for her childish behavior. She was the second-youngest child in a large and divided family. Sarah lived with her mother and stepfather, three of the stepfather's older children, and a younger child who was the daughter of Sarah's mother and stepfather. In this large and diversely related family, she often felt isolated and alone. She did not really remember her father, whom she had not seen since she was three years old; and she was not at all close to her stepfather, who was often away on business.

Sarah went to a school that stressed excellence in academic work. Identified as a "gifted child," she was under a great deal of pressure both at school and at home to achieve academically. Yet with no real sense of closeness to her father, Sarah did not know how to discipline herself nor did she wish to achieve academically, as her family and teachers expected. She rebelled in the only way she could: by acting silly, childishly and irresponsibly. The more adults disapproved of this behavior, the more isolated and rebellious she felt, and the more impelled to act childishly. Caught in this vicious circle, Sarah felt rejected by her family, her teachers and her peers.

She was a very bewildered little girl when, at her doctor's suggestion, she came to see me for counseling.

When I first met her, Sarah was rather withdrawn and uncommunicative. Apparently her mother had told her she was coming to see me so I could help her be a better student. No wonder Sarah was ill at ease. But as soon as she entered my playroom and saw the miniatures lining the walls, her whole personality changed. She seemed to forget her mother's expectations and, feeling very much at home, began creating a sand picture without even asking my permission.

Absorbed in this creative play, Sarah began to talk. While she did not want to talk much about herself, she obviously wanted to explain her sand picture to me. I told her some children make up stories that go along with their pictures. This prompted her to tell a story about the one she had just created, a first in a series of intricate adventures she would weave with ease. Sarah made up the following:

"Once upon a time there was a candy bag and in that bag there was something special. Nobody knew where the bag was and nobody knew there was something special in that bag. Then a boy found the bag and picked it up. He took it home and started to look inside, but even before he could peek, he was called to dinner. What was really in the bag was a tiny kitten, some gumdrops, a lollipop and some bubble gum. When the boy looked inside, he saw the kitten eating the gumdrops. He picked up the kitten and said, 'You cute little thing,' and took him downstairs to show his mother, his sister, his older sister and older brother. Then he showed them the candy. He asked, 'What shall I do with the kitten?'

"And little sister said, 'Let's keep him. We don't want him to die.' So they kept him and they lived happily ever after. They ate the candy. The End."

Sarah told this story very quickly; and, as soon as she had finished, she started telling me about her sand picture (Figure 23). Something in her voice connected me to her wishful longing to belong.

She explained that her sand picture had four different scenes in it, a big house in the center which she did not associate with any of the other four scenes. The scene in the northeast corner was a Christmas creche, depicting the birth of Jesus. She said, "I like this part best, about Jesus Christ, when he was born, with all of his friends and animals, too."

In the southeast corner of the box, Sarah placed the figure of an old lady whom she called a "witch." She said the witch had been shopping and had bought many things which she was now setting up to sell, hoping other people would buy them. My immediate intuition was that the merchant witch had something to do with

FIGURE 23

Sarah's image of her own mother; because I knew Sarah's mother was always busy shopping, buying various things for her large family or running errands for everyone. She seemed unable to say no to anyone.

All the horses in the south center belonged to "Mr. Peter" and a "Mrs. Piggle Wiggle." Horses are an important universal symbol for girls and, as a source of energy, no doubt represent the instinctive or more animal-like side of the individual. Apparently Sarah was not yet ready to claim this animal side in herself, because she said the horses belonged to other people. Sarah said one of the people who owned horses was Mrs. Piggle Wiggle, a character in a series of children's books. She is a very magical sort of lady who helps the children in her neighborhood with their problems: if they are having trouble with their schoolwork, she shows them how to study better; if they are messy at home, she teaches them to be neat. By saying Mrs. Piggle Wiggle owns the horses in this picture, Sarah was perhaps showing an early understanding of the instinctual or animal side of her own nature as a helpful side. Furthermore, getting in touch with her instincts would help her solve her own problems, especially if Mrs. Piggle Wiggle, her friend and therapist, helped.

In the northwest corner, Sarah's scene was of some animals enjoying themselves in the swimming pool. This fun, secret side was important to Sarah, and she subsequently put a similar scene in every sand picture she made.

The last scene, in the southwest part of the box, is a zoo. The last thing Sarah did was place a small squirrel eating an acorn seed just outside the zoo scene. Referring to the squirrel, she said, "He is so cute and pretty and fun; and he is free." She seemed to have a real feeling for this animal, as though it expressed a very important part of herself. As long as one is cute and free perhaps one won't be forced into "A" grades only. When she spoke of adding the acorn seed, I felt she just might be more in touch with her feminine side than she was rationally sure of or wanted to admit now (I am thinking of seeds as a universal feminine symbol of fertility and creative life).

At first I was not sure about the meaning of Sarah's elaborate first picture and story, but I paid careful attention to everything she said about this first scene. She was happily surprised to find an adult who recognized and respected the importance of this imaginary world. I realized later it told the story of her own life in four different parts.

The most important scene to Sarah was the one of the Christmas creche. Her family was Mormon; religion was an important part of her life. She seemed to have a deeply religious side, but she resented the many laws she had to follow and the long services she had to attend. In her later sand pictures, Sarah showed how she got more in touch with the beautiful and mysterious sides of her inner religion and spirit.

On her second visit to me, Sarah made a sand picture and told another story. Like the first, it was delivered in a kind of quick singsong voice which had a dream-like quality to it. This time she coordinated the story and picture; the figures resembled her own family. Her second picture contained important symbols, people and actions that are different from those in her first sandtray. For example, in the southwest side her father is depicted plowing a field with his teenage son; a scarecrow is there to protect the crops. In the northwest corner is a large tree with a very large owl peering out (the owl is a most important symbol for Sarah, and I will discuss this later when she talks more about it). The secret pond is again included, but this time three fish are swimming and three turtles are watching. A very large dog is watching and playing with the children. Sarah said two babies were playing together with a little elf man, and I felt she identified with this scene, which she carefully centered in the south of the tray. She also placed a very old man and woman near the children—most children would call them grandparents, but Sarah did not. She did say the domestic animals— cows, horses and pigs—needed to be penned up; and she placed white fences around them and then put the very large rooster to watch over all the animals. The animals occupied all of the east side of the box. Apparently Sarah felt the family was working and playing together and that the animals were important too. In any case, when she left, she told me how happy it made her feel to come to see me.

In her third sand picture, she made a lovely scene which she called "A Nature Scene" (Figure 24). She placed a royal leopard (which she called a princess) and its baby in an elaborately decorated cart which she made from a small blue boat. She gave the cart wheels and strings that harnessed two glass horses. A third horse walks alongside the cart. Sarah did not harness him. "He is free," she said. She told me that "The princess is feeling the wind and life outside." This scene, too, was filled with animals, most of them wild and playing freely; the picture shows animal families playing in nature. In the northeast side of the picture is the home of the lions and lionesses, with the same kind of little secret pond and ducks nearby. In the north center of the tray is a baboon family with a family of elephants playing nearby.

FIGURE 24

Another important part of this picture for Sarah is the hunter, who is standing near a big tree which has a large owl and another large bird perched in its branches. She placed this scene in the southeast corner of the sandtray. This is the second time she used the big owl, and she continued to use this and the hunter in many of her future pictures. It seemed as if Sarah somehow understood what animals playing freely and happily must feel about the threat of the hunter, who may put a permanent stop to their freedom. In a later picture, and with an accompanying story, Sarah really explored this figure of the hunter, and perhaps her own fear of losing her freedom.

In her fourth picture (Figure 25), Sarah shows hunters training and caring for animals in a circus. There are two rings or circles containing the animals and tamers. In the right or east circle are families of polar bears, brown bears and some pandas. The trainer in this circle is the same huntsman that Sarah used in her earlier scene. She said that "Here he cares for the animals." In the left or west circle are more violent animals-lions, a cheetah and some tigers — with a strong Prussian soldier training and keeping them in place. The soldier, like the huntsman, is an obvious symbol for authority and the dictates of society, but his authority is stronger than the huntsman's. By using him in a constructive way, Sarah shows she may now realize that some laws can help society by keeping real violence in check. These two carefully prepared circles as the containers may have indicated Sarah's growing awareness of the two sides of herself.

FIGURE 25

Behind the circus circles she placed many trees, with the very large owl in one. I was puzzled when she announced the owl had been shot, stuffed and placed in the tree, overlooking all the action. However, later I realized it was quite necessary to shoot and stuff the false day owl so it might be reborn as a true night owl. The real owl is a night or lunar animal; certainly he did not belong in this day scene. Sarah seemed to know this somehow, because she used the owl in many of her later scenes, always pointing out it was nighttime.

Whatever the symbolic meanings in this sand picture, it was a very important one for Sarah. Just as she could now separate the natural habitat of the bird, so could she separate her own instinctual feelings, and understand the place for her fantasies as well. As if to make this clearer, Sarah lined up the seven dwarves plus two miners along the front or south edge of the box, then placed a girl on horseback leading the parade of other horses and dwarves. Dwarves are subterranean working people as well as belonging to the world of fantasy. I felt Sarah seemed to realize how important it was that women keep close touch with the inside and magical side of life to balance life outside and above-ground, the rational and often mechanical world.

Sarah's next picture was another one of nature. Although quite detailed, her accompanying story is interesting enough to include here. In this story, Sarah tells much about her life and especially her confusion after her mother's remarriage, a feeling which was intensified by the fact that the two had lived alone for many years before her mother remarried. Sarah's story is as follows:

"The animals are having a meeting. They are talking about when the man is coming to destroy their houses. These were friendly wild animals; it is like lots of friends living together. Now some walked away, because they did not care what the king was saying as he is really bad. He had killed the real king, and the mother queen is glad. She likes him, but the other animals do not like this and do not want to obey him. That is why they walked away. It's the law though, for animals to obey the king.

"Mrs. Owl is very wise. She knows the bad king killed the other king even though she did not hear and see it. The killer king is this very bad, jealous lion. The wife knew they had killed the king; she is very mean to all the animals. The husband wanted her to be the Queen of the Forest, but she really lied to him.

"One of the rangers came. He hears a big noise. Men were being attacked and if the lion came closer, he would have killed him. The bears and all were watching and did not like this at all. The forest was no longer pleasant. It kept going on and it did not stop. This was the first time the animals really listened. They did not like what the men were doing; so the animals charged.

"Three men are killed, but no animals. Men on horses are coming out. They are trying to stop this. No one knows what is happening. What *is* happening??? "We have our rights, too. It keeps going on and on and on...," and birds and animals are chattering and chattering.

"The animals hated the people who came with Roman costumes on. The shiny costumes hurt their eyes. The men were stopping some of the animals but the animals were defeating them in some other ways. Finally, all the bears and everybody were going back to their homes. They did not want to watch, but some birds had to look and see. They decided they would have to get used to looking at such awful things."

"Mr. Owl had sent a mockingbird to say, 'Stop, Stop, Stop, Stop!' The lion charged. The elephants were stampeding. Even the boar was running into the bears' homes. Now the last of all the Roman soldiers were killed. The apes and the monkeys were chattering unhappily.

"Some of the animals kept fighting. They would not stop. Some went home and so did some men. The big birds stayed close to the water so they could duck their heads in when they could. The mockingbird still called, 'Stop, stop, we should not fight.' Mother kangaroo was terrified. She did not know what to do with her babies. Some of the men were still checking the forest. Some of the men put their guns away, but some kept them.

"Animals were going home. The lion was glad his wife was there, 'You will always be queen of the jungle.' But the jungle kept on with the noise, noise, noise. The mockingbird was ready to die.

"The apes kept chattering, 'Why can't it be a peaceful jungle without men?' The leader of the group was back with the squirrels, 'We must stop the families from fighting anymore. Have your decided anything, man?' 'You may be happy to know that we are figuring out a way out of this.'

"The squirrels are making up their minds. The mockingbird keeps saying, 'Stop, stop. You are wrecking our homes. Please, please stop! Our homes! Our homes! Don't you realize?'

"Mrs. Kangaroo says maybe they will listen if you keep flying around once more. The giraffes were shy and kept trying to hide all of the time. Finally, the mockingbird said, 'You must stop! Now!!'

"The man said, 'Stop this!' He went to the water and saw the animals were peaceful. 'I wish the lion had never started this fight with Man.' The mockingbird kept saying, 'You are foolish, please stop!' Men on horses got all of the animals to go home. So the Man left the pond. He had no business there. The deer found a good place, safe, in the rocks. Finally, the forest calmed down and the men all went away. This lovely forest in Monterey was quiet as could be. Never again was there fighting here. Some horses were left; that did not matter.

"'Make sure all the animals are in their homes,' said Mrs Lion. She can be trusted now!

The End."

At the end of the story, the mother lion can be trusted because she and the other female animals will no longer allow the interloper, man, into the forest. In real life, Sarah feared men and felt that as authoritarians they would destroy her carefully built world of fantasy and absorb her mother's love. The only way to deal with this threat was to refuse to compromise, to throw men out of the world.

However, as her story shows, Sarah begins to realize men do not need to be kicked out of the forest, that both she and her mother can live in a world with men, such as the one created by the remarriage. Now Sarah had to learn to understand both the masculine side of herself and the actual role of fathers as not only arbiters of law and order but as protectors in the big world outside. She starts moving in this direction when, towards the end of the story, she has a man ask the animals to stop fighting and go home. Just as Sarah has the animals look at the awful things that are happening, so she must now look at the beautiful and the ugly in her own world. If one of woman's roles is to be mediator to creativity, she needs to know all sides of herself. In this way, she will be able to express herself clearly. Separation comes when we lose touch with this knowledge and begin creating for its own sake. This inevitably leads to fighting and destruction, as Sarah describes in her story. First one must trust, but then one needs to use all the knowledge, strength and feeling possible to stop the fighting and bring harmony. Sarah seemed to know this, young as she was.

Sarah seemed to realize that animals, and some animal instincts, must be freed. In her next sand picture (Figure 26) she freed the horses. After pounding and patting and wetting the sand for a long time, angrily, she took every horse I had and placed them in the sandtray. She was silent for a while longer. Then she told me this

FIGURE 26

was a desert scene. She then grouped many sea shells and called them water holes. Some small trees protected the horses from the sun. She carefully chose some rocks and placed them around the scene as well.

This desert scene seemed to me to be primarily a setting for the horses, a place where they could be free. I felt they were somehow connected to Sarah's own instincts. When she finally told me the horses were free, she no longer pounded and wetted the sand. As the horses were free, Sarah too seemed more relaxed and open. In fact, she seemed especially happy as she left that day.

Sarah's next sand picture, a Christmas scene, was again about rebirth and new freedom. Although it was November, I felt the scene had more than a seasonal significance. While it depicted the birth of Christ, I felt it also symbolized an important internal birth of Sarah's own personality.

In her next picture (Figure 27), which she called "A Special Day," Sarah lit a candle in the center of the sandtray. I felt it symbolized the light burning inside Sarah. Men and women are working in front of the candle. One old peasant couple, the same grandparents as in Sarah's first picture, are in the south center of the sandtray. In the southwest corner of the tray, near the couple, two large dogs and some children are playing. Sarah asked if she could break the petals off some orange and yellow plastic flowers to make them look like planted corn and squash; then she carefully planted these in straight rows in the west side of the tray. The plants really looked like growing vegetables. A man was driving a horse-drawn plow over the ground. Sarah then put up the same scarecrow figure she had used before in the center of the rows to protect the crops.

FIGURE 27

The domestic animals were again placed in pens in the northeast corner of the tray. But Sarah left one gate in the fence open. On the right or east side of the tray a large rooster watches over the women who are feeding the fowl.

Having completed this scene, Sarah then lit the candle. She said that because man had invented something special, the candle was lit to celebrate and to show appreciation for what he had done. "You must respect him," she said. Then, in a deep, chanting voice, Sarah began to half-sing and half-recite the following:

"Your cows will be penned up,"
"Your pigs will be penned up,"
"Your horses will be penned up."
"You will all work and not stop until the end of the day."
"You will all buy a parrot."

"To buy a parrot" could be just Sarah's sense of humor or her impatience at listening to some of the long sermons she told me about. Then Sarah changed her tone of voice to a lighter and higher monotone and half-whispered the following:

"The rooster is over the cows; the rooster is over the cows. The little boy is looking at the pigs. Others are caring for the dogs. A sacred candle is in the center, because it is a special day."

Sarah continued her chanting, but so quickly I could not quite write it all down. She sang something like, "Each family has two families." And she added some words like, "Plow your corn. Water your squash."

Her song conveyed Sarah's understanding of the entire order of nature. She seemed to know that men must take care of women and that both men and women must feed and water the animals and tend the crops. Sarah sensed it is woman's secret and sacred joy to nourish life within herself as well as to care for all the living things in the world outside.

After this beautiful "Special Day" picture, I was at first surprised to see that Sarah's next picture (Figure 28) was a very different scene which she called "ugly." Later I recognized this as a good sign: it told me that Sarah could accept and understand both the beautiful and the ugly. At the time, I felt Sarah might have tried to make an ugly scene because she had some resentment and anger which she had to let out that day. Her mother had come with her to talk to me. I suggested Sarah make a sand picture while her mother and I talked. Sarah may have felt she was being shoved aside for part of what was her own hour.

The prehistoric scene was very creatively done. As in many of Sarah's pictures, there was a lovely watering place, a sort of pond, in the northwest corner of the tray. This picture was especially interesting to me because girls rarely use the figures of prehistoric animals. However, Sarah used these animals in a manner quite different from the ways in which boys use them. Generally, boys show these animals fighting or sometimes mating. Sarah had the dinosaurs paired off in families, caring for each other and for their young. This confirmed my observations that boys and girls work very differently in the sand.

After this prehistoric scene, Sarah returned to making pictures having more to do with family themes. Her next picture had all the elements of her own inner symbolism. In the left or west corner

FIGURE 28

of the tray she placed some horses behind a fence, and said that a little girl was taking her father to see them. This seemed to be quite an important element in the scene. It seemed that Sarah realized the inner, instinctual importance of these animals to the little girl. The fact that the girl is taking her father to see the horses is also important. Apparently, the little girl in the picture wants to communicate something of her inner energy to her father. Perhaps Sarah was beginning to realize how important communication between a girl and her father can be.

Also significant is the little boy who is taking his mother to see some trains, which are in the northeast corner of the tray. Perhaps Sarah realizes here that it is important for the boy to communicate his inner force and movement to his mother. Sarah may even realize there are two sides to herself: an outer energy side and an inner instinctual side. Both sides need to be communicated with and understood.

Her hidden fantasy world is also in this picture. She has grouped some children and dwarves around a castle. The last thing she did was to place a large totem pole in the southwest corner of the tray, and two large trees towards the center in the south. The totem pole is certainly an inner symbol, showing something of Sarah's growing awareness of the strength in her own hidden inner world. The large trees might symbolize that strength as alive and growing.

Sarah now felt free enough to make more of her "ugly" scenes; she felt safe to communicate more of her primal instinctual side. She said her next picture, which she called "The Ungo Bungo Men," (Figure 29) was a "goopey." And it really was, for she literally drenched the sand while making the scene.

There is much aggression as well as humor in this scene. Again, she made a large water hole in the center of the tray. In the northeast corner, she placed some yellow and black figures which she called cavemen. She built a strong cave for them out of rocks, and placed guards on top of it to watch over them. In front of the cave Sarah placed some tiny prairie dogs. She said one of them had slipped away from the protection of the cave and had been eaten by wild animals. She put some plants around for food, and a large bowl of water in the center of the picture. One prehistoric animal stood inside the bowl, several other animals appeared on the left or southwest corner of her scene.

FIGURE 29

In the northwest corner, she built a wall of sand and put some prehistoric animals and a pterodactyl inside it. She kept wetting the wall, saying it felt so good. In the southeast corner, Sarah placed more carnivorous prehistoric animals and standing bears. She then said that most of the animals must be penned up for their own protection.

Sarah said this was "ugly," like pictures boys would make. I asked if she felt all her pictures had to be pretty and why boys only made ugly scenes. Sarah thought for a while. Wary about answering questions, she then confided that her parents had asked her about our work together. She also told me she was being tested at school again. I was glad Sarah could verbalize more of her external problems.

Actually, Sarah's academic work had begun to improve markedly. Maybe being able to play freely in the sand had helped her mark off time for play and time for work. She seemed better able to concentrate on her schoolwork, to know when it was appropriate to be serious about work.

"The Ungo Bungo Men," with its free expression of instincts, proved to be a real turning point for Sarah. Her subsequent pictures showed quite clearly her own developing instinctual side and a true differentiation in her own personality.

The next picture (Figure 30) has two fairly high hills in it, with a water jug concealed inside the one on the left or western side. Circling around the left hill are black and white horses. A mother and a father tiger, somewhat protected by a large tree, are mating in front of the hill. A family of polar bears stands on the hill in the right or eastern side.

FIGURE 30

Between the two hills Sarah put a very large tree, with two ponies and a mountain goat standing behind it. Behind the hills she placed more mountain goats and a small mouse in a nesting hole. Sarah then melted some red wax in front of the hill on the right, an interesting addition. She explained it represented blood, although no fighting or violence took place. This small pool of red wax or blood seemed to have something to do with her developing puberty, which she was just beginning. Sarah was clearly separating and defining sexual and instinctual roles for herself in this picture. Obvious masculine and feminine sexual symbolism seem self-explanatory.

Both these symbols and those in her next picture showed she was becoming quite knowledgeable and comfortable with both spiritual and bodily sexual symbols, no longer needing to split her body-mind thinking and feeling.

Sarah's next picture (Figure 31) represented the feminine side of human nature beautifully, and seemed linked to her last picture. This one also contains two scenes. On the right or east side she built some troughs in the sand, which she said were feeding pens for horses and cows. She then placed a fence partway around them to protect the animals from the fighting with the Arabs which she said was going on in this picture.

The second scene, on the left or west side, consists of a small circle molded in the sand. A tree with red flowers stands in the left-center of this circle. Small horses, mostly white, circle the tree. The entire circle, with the small red tree in the center, closely resembles a small breast.

Whether Sarah realized her figure looked like a breast is not too important. What is important is that the whole picture is about the feminine role of feeding and nourishing others; the breast, clearly traced in the sand, symbolizes Sarah's feelings.

Sarah scattered red wax around this picture too, again symbolizing blood. Sarah seems quite aware of the feminine role: that a woman feeds and nourishes others with joy, and that this constant nourishing is always accompanied by pain.

When I looked at the slide later, I quite clearly saw a small, embryolike face traced in the sand near and just south of the feeding pens. This strange face and "half body" form another feeding pen that looks very much like the partial body of a small child. This aspect clearly expressed Sarah's awareness of woman's reproductive function and of her own birth and rebirth, that endless cycle inherent in all our lives.

I saw this sense of rebirth manifesting itself in Sarah's life outside of treatment. She was certainly beginning to separate her own psyche from her parents and their demanding wishes. She no longer felt so pressured to excel at school; as a result, her academic work began to improve because she was more relaxed about it. In essence, Sarah was growing up; she was becoming her own person, and her peers saw this also. Even she could now admit to me that many of her classmates liked her, instead of always complaining that no one did.

Her next sand pictures reflect this growing integration and good feeling about herself. Every one of them was creative and clear. She made many more family and farm scenes. Then she made a very

FIGURE 31

moving picture filled with energy which she called "A Happy Day."
In the background, to the north, a lot of construction is going on,
no doubt symbolizing the constructive forces in her own life. A train
was coming into the construction area. Toward the center of the
picture, cows and horses were walking along a road. This picture
was about arrival, about rebuilding, about new life.

This exuberant mood is shown most clearly in the horse-racing
scene she built in the front center of the tray. The track is surrounded
by fenced-in galleries filled with spectators. A male timekeeper stands
on the southeast side of the race track and two women riders are
lining up to race. I was interested to see that the women are racing
and the man is keeping time. It seems that Sarah is now racing toward
life. Man had always symbolized for her the strictures of society,
but in this picture she takes these strictures into account, no longer
feeling bound or inhibited by them. Although the man will keep
time, Sarah will race in her own way. I feel strongly now that Sarah's
life will always be an active one, full of movement and people, and
that along with all this activity she will maintain her perspective.

She then made another picture, a more quiet one expressing some
of her growing spiritual or inner integration, which had developed

along with her growing outer integration. She called this last scene "Visiting Chinatown" (Figure 32). Physical activity and outer life in this picture are again represented by two riders, a man and a woman, she said, near a fence, with a gate to the right in the exact center of the tray. The horsemen are not racing, but are lined up outside the fence looking, with other spectators, at two Buddhas in the north center. Even the most active elements seem to be taking time out to sit still, contemplate the Buddhas and think about spiritual things. The old wise Chinaman whom she calls a fisherman in her story is placed in the east center. She has again included her magic pond, which is in the southeast corner. There are ducks, pelicans and swans around the pond, and fish inside it. Sarah has also included the same magical totem north of the fence. The King and Queen of the story she tells about this picture are also sitting north of the fence, with a bird placed between them. Near the Buddha is a small cat placed near a tree.

FIGURE 32

Sarah's story about this picture is fairly complex and very rich in symbolism. She tells us:

"It's a Chinese scene; the King and Queen are out. A girl is watching the tree and trying to get her cat to come back. There are lots of pretty birds by the pond. It was a happy fun day. There is a purple, blue and white bird that lives alone.

"There were beautiful, beautiful flowers everywhere. That day, the fisherman was talking to the Princess. Two Chinese people just sat and looked at the Buddha. There is a pool that represents the Chinese, and a totem pole.

"On the way, some men were working on the road. They did not like it, but the law said they must; so they went on doing it. It was a happy day. Cars kept coming in. Workmen were annoyed with all the cars and trucks and confusion.

"The birds were getting frightened. The swan's babies were just born and she did not know what to do. Someone called and the train came in. It would stay there always, so that they would know the exact space at all times. A man and woman on horseback came too.

"Finally, the largest bird went away, and he flew and flew and never came back. Then the purple birds flew away. The babies stayed. They wanted to see the King and Queen. Midget's house is being constructed, so he moved to a small house right next to the Queen—he is very lucky. All had said, 'Can I have that house?' And they said, 'No.' It was for midgets to walk into and not pay rent. The gate was small, but China people are small.

"The fisherman was kicked out of his house because he could not pay the rent, so he went to the pond to look at the fish. The birds and fish did not act scared; he did not want to catch them. The tall fisherman kept saying, 'It is not fair—I want the free house.' They liked the man and were sorry, but knew what was right and what was wrong."

This is certainly a fairy story, but it is a serious story, too. All of Sarah's stories seem to be about the conflict between society and the individual. Her first stories were more confused in their resolution of this conflict, but in this story the resolution seems clear. Sarah recognizes the rules of society, that there are laws which must be respected even when they seem to be unfair. The tall fisherman is the free man in the story. He knows it is unfair for the King and Queen to give the midget the small house for free, but there is nothing he can do about it. The fisherman wants to keep his freedom, and in order to do so he must conform to the rules of the King and Queen, whether he likes them or not.

There is some sadness in Sarah's story. She knows what growing up means now. Sometimes, you may be unhappy when you live in society. Only the birds are free to leave when they choose. And Sarah knows that she is not a bird. She, like the fisherman, must conform to some rules she may not like. And like the fisherman, she will continue to cherish her fantasy world and her inner freedom, but try to keep this side separate from society and its rules.

Religion gives Sarah great strength, helping her keep her sense of the beauty of life intact, no matter how unfair the demands of society may seem to her. The Buddhas and the flowers provide beauty for everyone in this story, even for the unhappy girl who is searching for her cat, and for the fisherman who does not want to conform.

Sarah seems to be in touch with eternal time when she says the train will always stay there so they will know the exact space at all times.

We were approaching the right time for Sarah and me to separate. But she asked to make two more sand pictures. At first I was not sure why, but afterwards it became clear that they were an important final statement for Sarah.

She called the first picture "A Town of Little People" (Figure 33); the second, "A Town." Both are rather similar. However, "Little People" is more carefully made and shows more activity. Again, the church—symbolically, religion—is in the center. Sarah then smoothed the sand very carefully. "To make it safe for the little people," she said. Safety and security seem to be the theme of this picture. The train symbolizes connection, as she clearly explained in her last story about Chinatown, when even in the midst of a chaotic party the train calmly waited at the station.

FIGURE 33

Sarah remembers to include a building filled with food supplies for the time of winter snows so that the people will be fed and cared for. She also includes her magic pond, full of water for the animals. Even a well organized and civilized community has its magic.

"A Town," Sarah's last picture, is very simple, with much the same theme of "Little People," but more like the community in which Sarah actually lives. The gas station and the big house seem necessary in suburbia. Sarah does not need to pen up the animals any more. At least they can be free and go to the barn for protection from the cold when needed. Sarah seems to understand that freedom and society can work hand in hand to provide security and, at the same time, happiness.

Instead of the pond, Sarah put a watering pen for the animals. Even the magic pond now has a function in providing the much-needed water. Sarah says there is a place here, too, for the storage of food and supplies so no one will go hungry in the winter. Maybe it was her way of saying goodbye to me: "My community is strong now; but if the snows come, I will need food and supplies I have stored away."

9

ATTEMPTED SUICIDE AND REBIRTH

Susi was fourteen when she attempted suicide by taking a large amount of aspirins and other pills. As she had told no one she took the pills until she became so ill she could not function, much of the poison had entered her bloodstream by the time she reached the hospital. The doctors were quite concerned for her life at first; however, Susi survived after she was given emergency treatment. In the hospital she was given crisis help, and then it was suggested to Susi that she come to me for further counseling.

Susi was a member of a large family which had recently moved from a large city to a more rural area. Church was a very important part of family life for them, and through their church activities most of Susi's family had made new friends after the move.

However, this was not the case with Susi. She was very lonely after the move. The new neighborhood had no girls or boys near her age, and she had found no friends in church. Before the family moved, Susi had a number of friends in a drama group. She appeared to have a real feeling for dramatics.

Although she was quite intelligent, Susi was not very interested in school. Susi was shy and did not like to be called on in class. She was at an age when most people are confused about growing up and what it means. Susi liked to stay by herself a lot to think things out. Most of all, she liked to read.

This quietness did not make Susi very noticeable, either at home or at school. As a member of such a large family, Susi often felt ignored. Her parents seemed to be genuinely concerned for Susi's welfare, but did not quite know how to express this concern to her in a constructive way. The parents seemed to have a good relationship with each other, and to manage well with such a large family. They showed real pride in family unity and were very much concerned that Susi felt left out of the family group. The suicide attempt had shocked and frightened them and made them realize that they were not communicating with their daughter at all. They did not seem to know how to reach her.

As I worked with Susi and had a few meetings with her parents, we all reached a better understanding. Susi's parents gained more insight into her feelings, especially her feelings of loneliness. They became more loving toward them in return.

I had been told most of Susi's history before she came to me. When I first met her, however, her posture and her way of speaking told me much more about her than I had learned from hearing her history. Susi walked using a stooped posture and a halting gait. When she sat down, on her first visit, she kept fidgeting with her dress and moving her hands nervously. The dress was rather low-cut and she seemed to be trying to continually cover up her small developing breasts. Susi made it clear to me that she did not like to talk, but preferred to sit and read by herself. During our first visit, she did manage one small smile, which made her seem much more alive and attractive.

When one of her parents called me into the waiting room on that first visit, I suggested to Susi that she might want to make a sand picture while I was busy. I certainly was not prepared for the very complete picture she made in so short a time.

Susi made a picture showing a community which was full of activity. She chose a large train station and placed it on the west side of the sandbox, with at least twenty tiny figures of people standing outside the station, waiting for the train. On the south side of the train station, Susi put a bench with one man sitting on it. Along the southern edge of the box, she fenced in groups of cows, pigs and other animals, and showed people feeding them. On the eastern edge of the box, Susi placed two houses. One was unfinished and had people working on its construction. There were other figures of people working in the fields around the house. In the exact center of the box, Susi placed a church, and next to it another unfinished house. A small house with a water wheel, placed in the northwest corner of the box, completed the picture.

The intricacy and beauty of Susi's first sand picture helped tell me her trust for me was immediate. Apparently I was right: the next time Susi came to see me, she talked a great deal. She told me about a boy she liked—but each time he came over, her younger brother monopolized his attention by insisting on playing rough boy games. Susi was sure this boy liked her too, but she did not know how to handle the friendship. I asked her if she had talked to her father about her brother and she said, no, she felt he would not understand. She also told me about girls she'd like to be friends with. She said most girls thought her too young and shy. We talked about different ways of making friends. Susi also told me her parents liked the younger children better than her; she herself felt one brother was very talented in art and one sister a much better student than she.

On subsequent visits, Susi made a few more pictures in the sand. Once she painted a picture of herself as a little girl with a very red face and no hands (Figure 34). Looking at this picture, I thought Susi was trying to know herself better. She called her painting "ugly," but seemed pleased with it nonetheless, and placed a ribbon in the girl's hair.

FIGURE 34

After painting this, Susi told me she did not want to use the sandtray any more because it made her fingernails dirty, and often she was going to see one of her friends after her session with me. I was happy to know that Susi was making friends in her new home. One boy had invited her to a party, and this was especially nice since she had been wanting him to like her for a long time.

Although she did not want to get her fingernails dirty, one day Susi went to the sandtray without a word and started to play. I believe that the sand picture she made at this time (Figure 35) was very important for Susi, and was responsible for much of the healing process which took place in our subsequent sessions together. Susi was very brave and open when she made this picture, for in it she really reenacted her own suicide attempt. It was a realistic picture about death and burial, and the process of reincarnation that occurs when one wants to live, not die. Sharing this picture was a very moving experience for both of us, difficult to describe. I can really only talk about the picture itself and what it looked like.

Susi first asked if I had some miniature figures she could use as gravestones. I found some wooden posts, which looked like blocks, and she liked these. She then very carefully dug graves, placed the figures of people in these holes, covered each grave with sand, and carefully indented the sand in front of each headstone to show exactly where the grave was. All the graves were on a higher mound of sand in the lower west part of the box.

Then Susi did something which really startled me. She asked if she might use a lovely china plate with intricate gold-plate designs on it. This plate had hardly ever been used in the sand before. She half-buried the plate to the right of the graves, then turned the exposed part of the plate with her hand so that the gold designs caught the light and gleamed brightly. As she turned the plate,

FIGURE 35

Susi said it symbolized the "resurrection," and that it had the power to bring those buried on the hill back to life. As Susi turned the plate, the gleaming light seemed quite powerful, almost hypnotizing. The plate indeed seemed to become a powerful light much like the sun.

At this point, Susi placed in the sand the figures of a man and a woman, whom she called a "mother" and a "father," and who were, she said, "looking for their lost child." She moved the figures over the box to show that these parents were searching. Then she buried the gold plate deeper in the sand, placed the figures of some workmen on top of the buried plate and showed them digging.

Susi then dug a water hole in the sand to the rear and east of where the workmen were digging. She quietly and slowly uncovered the buried plate and moved it around again to catch the light. As she did this, Susi uncovered some of the buried people. One of them was a little girl. She said that when the men had found the plate, they had found the lost child as well. The plate symbolized for her the power of resurrection; when it had been found, most of the people on the hill came back to life.

Susi had been able to share with me some of her feelings about taking the pills before she made this picture. She really did not want to die, but was willing to take the chance if it was the only way her parents would notice her. She told me many times there seemed to be little to live for. When she brought the little girl back to life in her picture, we both said very little; we both knew what Susi meant to say with this picture and action in the sandtray.

We were both very moved and silent for a long time. After a while, I think I said something about life and death and renewal. It seemed to be the right thing to say, because Susi smiled a lovely and open smile. We hugged and everything seemed all right at the moment.

How the sand works is still a great mystery to me. Was it the sun's light that shone on the Chinese plate which helped heal Susi? I do not really know, but it seemed that she was healed from some of the very deep wounds of the suicide attempt. I did not see Susi many more times after she made this picture. The family said they were still close enough to me to call me if I were needed. I was concerned, however, that they broke off therapy too soon, but Susi's father said that they just could not afford to continue.

I have kept in touch with Susi and her family. Susi herself has become much more involved in life, has made quite a few girl friends and participates in church activities. She no longer feels her problems to be so different from those of other girls; she is invited to slumber parties and dances with her friends. She seems, in general, to have realized that her path in life is not so very different from the paths of others, as she had imagined.

To be healed, Susi had to get back in touch with her instincts, especially her instinct for life. She had to stop and listen to herself, and to make herself understood by others. The suicide attempt was part of that fight. But Susi was only fighting, not listening; nor was anybody listening to her. The sand pictures helped her really see who she was. They showed her the love of life which she had abundantly within herself. When Susi came in touch with this creative part of herself, she began to like herself better and to be her own friend. Then it was easier for her to move from this friendship with herself to a real friendship with others. I feel that instead of always retreating or fighting, Susi can now stop and listen, and other people can and will listen to her in return.

10

RESOLUTION OF FAMILY PROBLEMS

Jill was thirteen years old when she came to me. Her mother, concerned about Jill's relationship with her stepfather, sent her to see me. In the three years since her mother remarried, Jill had not related well to her stepfather. Also, she did not seem to have much feeling of closeness to the two babies born to her mother since the remarriage. The only close tie Jill had, according to her mother, was with an eighteen-year-old sister who lived with Jill's father and his second wife in another town, and thus who seldom saw Jill.

Jill seemed to be open with me from the first. She liked to talk about herself, her school and her family. From the beginning she also enjoyed working in the sandtray.

A child's sand picture can be an expression of a personal myth as well as a playful attempt to get to know the sandtray and its possibilities. This was the case with Susi's first picture of a community. It was also true of Jill, whose first picture was a zoo scene. She put most of the animals in pens, with figures of people outside the pens watching the animals. A family of ducks and a swan beside a small pond and a tree were in the middle of the scene. A little girl was feeding them. These "special animals" were not penned up, Jill told me.

In the north or far side of the box was a pen with an elephant and a waterhole inside it. A sea lion was playing in the water, and there was a man cleaning up inside the pen. Jill placed a tall pine tree in the center of the pen.

In the northeast corner of the box, Jill set up a large, fenced-off den of polar bears and another complete family of bears with a cave and two trees for their home and protection. In the center of this was a gold plate filled with water. Two little bears played in the water. In the center of the east side of the box, Jill built another pen and put a variety of animals inside it: a zebra, some pigs, a parrot and a mountain goat. In the southeast corner is a family of lions.

Jill filled the west side of the sandbox with unusual animals in interesting groupings. In the northwest corner is a pen containing three snakes and a wild boar. Another special pen containing two giraffes and a bird, which she called a "king bird," is on the west side of the box.

When she completed the zoo scene, Jill quickly made another scene in the dry sand. To the right or east of this scene she placed the figure of a mother baboon with her baby. A very dark figure of a male baboon stood to one side of the mother and baby. She put the baboons in a pen by digging a sort of fence in the sand. She put some trees inside the pen with the baboon family.

To the left or west of this scene Jill put three baby bears, a tree and a rock. Then she dug a triangular pen for these bears. In the west corner she placed a large duck, a pelican, a penguin and some fish. She fenced these animals off with a white fence, and in the enclosure put some flowers, a mirror-pond, and a man working.

Jill left the central and eastern parts of the scene empty. After tracing some designs in this black sand, Jill announced she was finished.

Although these were only her first two sand pictures, they did show me some important aspects about Jill. She seemed to be trying to get in touch with some feelings just beneath the surface. At this point she was like the mirror-pond with the flowers on it: she presented a beautiful and friendly surface that was difficult to penetrate.

Most of these buried feelings had to do with families, with fathers and mothers and children. In her picture of the zoo, the animal families calmly playing on the east side of the box contrasted with the snakes and wild boars on the west side. It almost seemed that these dangerous animals were threatening the families. Perhaps Jill felt this threat and penned her animal families in so carefully because of it.

Jill seemed particularly confused about the male animals and their roles. In the baboon family scene, the male baboon is standing off to one side, almost threatening the mother baboon and her baby. In the zoo scene, Jill put all the workmen figures together with the animals and carefully penned them in, as if the men were somehow as dangerous as the animals in the cages. Only the little girl outside a pen is allowed to roam freely with the few peaceful animals who are not fenced in. From these two sand scenes it seemed that Jill felt some anxiety about the stability of the family, and that she felt somehow threatened by father figures, or men.

On her first visit, Jill did not want to talk much, so there was no way for me to verify my intuitions about her. To help her get in touch with herself, I asked Jill on her second visit if she would like to paint. She responded enthusiastically and made two pictures.

Her first picture was of a sunset. Her second depicted a green and blue flower between two large, embryo-like black images. A lovely orange color showed at the top of one of these black masses. The sunset picture was much more peaceful, showing a bright sunset on a sea filled with calm waves.

Jill liked the sunset picture and wanted to keep it. She said, however, that the flower picture was "ugly," and she left it with me. I was glad to have it because this picture told me a lot about Jill. I felt that she herself was a kind of flower, kept a child too long because of her family situation. The two black images suggested,

FIGURE 36

perhaps, her divided family, and how threatened Jill felt by this division. Since they are definitely in the shapes of embryos it seemed to me Jill was depicting the dark fear she was experiencing in separating herself from her parental images (See Figure 36).

The third time Jill came to see me, she talked quite a bit about her family, about her stepfather and her own father, and her relationship with each of them. Jill liked horses and she talked a lot about them. She seemed to relate really well to animals, and this knowledge made the zoo scene more understandable to me. During this visit, Jill asked me what a "lesbian" was. Apparently she had heard the term and did not want to ask her parents about it. This question had some significance later in her treatment, as Jill began to communicate to me worries she had about her feelings for some girls she babysat for and the two younger children of her mother and stepfather, who were both girls. These worries seemed understandable to me when I kept Jill's two fathers, and her confusion about them, in mind. It seemed that Jill needed an adequate male image, and had not yet really found one to identify herself with.

Jill made two sand pictures on this visit. The first, a pretty "play" scene, she called a birthday cake (Figure 37). She made a big mound of sand and placed a lighted candle on top of it, with another candle to the left or west of the box. She decorated the mound with

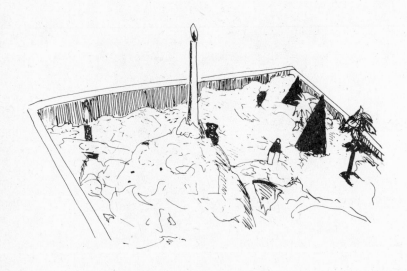

FIGURE 37

droppings of colored wax. On the right or east are five trees with a man crossing the bridge towards them. Just behind the main candle Jill placed a mother brown bear.

In her next picture, Jill took the figure of a man and called it her father. She then buried the figure in the sand, but quickly dug it up, feeling it would be better to have the "mother," a female figure which she placed next to the father, take care of him; she said the father was "ill." It seems that Jill's own father had been frequently ill, and that her mother had cared for him. Perhaps this illness strained the marriage. Jill worried about her father and about who was caring for him now that her mother was no longer with him.

On another visit, Jill made a lovely picture of a town with many animals (Figure 38), but unlike the zoo picture, here the animals are integrated into the life of the community. Animals always seemed to be important symbols for Jill. She needed to get in touch with her own animal instinct, with the hidden woman inside of her. For me, this was one of her "healing" pictures.

FIGURE 38

Jill first placed a row of houses on the west side of the tray, a church at the top of the row and woods to the north of it. She said that this row of houses was a "peaceful town with people." To the right or east of the box she placed a large house and two women approaching it on horseback. In the southeast corner, at the bottom of the box, Jill safely penned up some horses and cows so they would not wander onto the freeway, she said.

In the center of the sandtray, she built a hill with a tunnel through it. Then she made a road going through the tunnel and around the hill. The road passed by the town in the west, the large home in the northeast, and the cows and horses in the southeast corner. On the road were many trucks and cars and much movement. Jill said that this road was "the freeway." In fact, she frequently traveled on freeways with her family, and always when she came to see me. On the freeway overpass, Jill also put houses, trees and people. The entire picture showed movement and life. All the cars, trucks, people and animals seemed to be going somewhere, to have a purpose. Instead of having all of the animals penned up, as in the zoo picture, Jill had women riding the horses to a house. It seemed that the women had learned to use animals to a good purpose. These women on horseback showed me that Jill was no longer afraid of her instincts. She could now listen to them and use them to help her get in touch with herself and with other people, just as the women riders used the energy of the horses to help them reach a house with people in it.

This picture seemed to be very happy. I was not surprised to hear Jill's family say she was doing quite well at home and at school. She was happy with her friends, and seemed to like her baby sisters in a more gentle way. Apparently, Jill and her stepfather had made great progress in their communication. The happiest event for Jill at this time was that her eighteen-year-old sister was coming for a long visit during the summer. This had never happened before.

Jill came to see me a few more times. She made several nature scenes in the sandtray. One seemed especially important to me. She called it "a meeting of the animals." She let the animals out of their pens and allowed birds, rabbits and bears to play peacefully together in the center of the box. This scene showed me Jill's increasing integration. She was much more aware of her instincts, and this awareness made her feel more at home with herself.

Jill told me that she would like to drop out of treatment for the summer. She had many plans for things to do with her sister and her friends, and wanted to have her free time to herself. I had discussed this idea with Jill's mother, and I did not see any reason for Jill to continue treatment at present.

On her last visit to me, Jill seemed very relaxed. She just enjoyed playing in the sand. She talked a great deal about her family and friends and her plans to go to the beach with them in the summer.

This was not long-term therapy because Jill really had a strong ego and a basically stable personality from the first. The history of this therapy shows quite clearly, however, that Jill, like Susi, needed to come into touch with her own instinctual, intuitive side. When I stopped seeing Jill, she seemed to be at the point of integrating her instincts into her daily, conscious life. More than anything, she had needed someone to listen to her. Her own father had been ill and far away. She was separated from her older sister, and her mother often was so busy caring for the two younger children that she had little time for her. The new stepfather and the new babies seemed to confuse Jill, and she just needed someone to talk it over with. This was all in addition to the many problems all adolescents have in growing up.

Jill talked a good deal about her family with me. In making her sandtray pictures she also, in a sense, talked her confusion over with her own inner self. The needed symbols seemed to evolve for Jill almost from the beginning. She was aware of animal instinct and its energy. Her pictures were full of snakes, bears and wild boars. And, in the end, these animals changed and she herself seemed transformed. They became more tame and lived together peacefully, as Jill herself seemed able to do in her own family.

The birth of Jill's inner, flower-like self was well expressed in both of her paintings. She seemed to be instinctually aware that she was a woman, and of the beautiful and delicate instinctual side which this identity gave to her. Jill's instinct was always to integrate her inner flower self with the moving collective, the community. At the end of treatment, she seemed to be sure that she could balance her inner, secret self and its needs with the outer world of movement and people, and the demands and needs she found both expressed and fulfilled in this world. I shared Jill's confidence in her own inner balance and integration. I felt she was well on her road of knowing and experiencing a deeper form of relationship in life.

11

AN INNER JOURNEY INTO THE FEMININE
The Story of Mary As Told in Sand and Dreams

It seems only fitting to begin this final case study by explaining what I believe this uniquely healing, non-verbal, non-rational creative sandplay process is all about. Right now, with the upsurge of interest in working with molested children and adults, there is a very great interest in using the sandtray as a diagnostic and therapeutic tool. Unfortunately, it seems that some are using sandplay without much experience or training, and others in a more interpretive way than I am used to doing. Since my early training with Hal Stone, and especially with Dora Kalff in 1970, 1973, and 1976, I have followed what I call the "Jungian way." By this I mean that I believe in the importance of association and amplification and in the innate factors of healing, rather than in too much interpretation and reduction. Dr. Jung was always able to understand symbolic imagery and meaning—in other words, to hear the voice in the stones. He used symbols as the key, as images not signs. I agree—and thus for me, sandtray symbols do almost literally come alive.

Given a tray of sand and a set of miniature figures and objects, the individual creator's unconscious is allowed to direct his conscious action and to express itself symbolically. The emphasis is on non-verbal communication between one's own conscious and unconscious and those of the observer-therapist. I feel that in this meeting of conscious and unconscious—in a free and protected environment—the psyche tends to balance itself autonomously, and to unfold the individual's original, potential wholeness. However, I do agree with Estelle Weinrib when she says that it takes more than a tray with some sand, a collection of small objects, and a dictionary of symbols for this to happen.

The process that I follow in my work is practically the same with children as with adults, and I do find that some children go through a very deep individuation process when they are allowed to work freely and for some length of time. The case study I am presenting is, however, of an adult female, age 23. I will call her Mary. I feel that we shared a profound rapport in a protected space during our three and a half years of work.

Many of Mary's sandtrays seemed to be creative acts. Later on in the analytical process her dreams would often correlate and perhaps even amplify the sand pictures—or more often, the sand images would enlarge the dream images. I am very sure that her sand pictures helped build a bridge to the outer world, making her inner reality and external life work together and balance out, so to speak. I now *know* from my experiences with so many patients—and this of course includes Mary—that there is indeed a fundamental drive toward healing and wholeness in the psyche.

I believe it necessary to ask questions at different points in time, especially when viewing slides with a patient, and I often learn a great deal about how different miniatures may at different times evoke different symbols for the same person. It is essential to be in tune with the patient's view of the figures at all times; however, it is just as vital that one be allowed to venture somewhat silently into the darkness of the unconscious (matriarchal consciousness as well) on the path to full recovery. This seems especially necessary when someone has been cut off or not clearly bonded with the mother at an early age. It's obvious in Mary's case that a normal separation of her self from her mother may not have taken place, at least not at a very early age. Because of her sandplay and dream therapy, I feel that Mary was able to temporarily revert to a uroboric state in order to regain a sense of bonding—a sense which later, of course, had to be transferred back to her own mother, both inner and outer.

Certainly, Mary experienced matriarchal consciousness through sandplay by observing and being aware, by letting her feelings be affected by feeling and intuition. It has been said before, but I like to repeat, that if one hasn't had an experience one cannot explain it. I felt sure that Mary began to know herself as a totality and as the directing center, and to make some distinction between ego and self as moved and mover. One can see this process in Mary's sand pictures, especially in the later ones.

Mary first came to me to learn more about sandplay. She had heard one of my public lectures on Jungian psychology and sandplay, and had taken some courses in a graduate program in a San Francisco-area university. She told me she did not feel good about her work with her current therapist, and later brought me two or three dreams showing fairly clearly how she actually did feel. I have included one of these dreams later in the case study. I suggested she not break off her therapy immediately, but perhaps come to me and do a few trays so that we could come to a better and more considered decision. Her need for a "Jungian" connection and her confusion about what to expect from sandplay no doubt helps explain the rather unclear first two sandtray pictures she produced (see Figures 39 and 40 and all following later in the text).

When Mary made her third tray (Figure 41), I was naturally impressed with the beauty and depth she revealed, but I was also a little suspicious about a kind of "Jungian fascination" that was currently popular in many colleges. However, the few associations she shared with me did tell me she was sincere and in touch with some deep part of her psyche. Her comments were that she felt like the elephant — big and awkward, tottering on the two rocks, hesitating to dive into deep water. She also mentioned the dwarf-man as being very dignified and sure of life. I did not mention the beautiful mandala effect of the whole picture, since at that time I did very little talking during the therapy session. In any case I was sure she was aware of the effect. The image did in fact move both of us enough to know that we wanted to work together. I was very relieved when she asked if she might work in a more personal way with her own journey, using dreams and sand pictures. I am sure that she had at first wanted to get some sandplay training in order to use it later in her own practice. For now, though, she was able to know that she needed more personal therapy and much more clinical study and experience.

I need to say a few words about Mary's fourth sandtray (Figure 42), because looking back it was a real turning point for both of us. I was probably not too tactful in commenting that she should try to get a bit more into her play side (see Figures 41 and 42). Later on she told me that the fourth picture was partly a product of her anger towards me for that remark. At least I was able to see the humor, and anger too, of the little dog in the tree sticking its tongue out at everyone when a ball was squeezed. In Mary's mind, no doubt it was looking at me. Of course there is a great deal more in the picture, and it certainly gave her courage to realize what she really wanted and needed, and that was more therapy at a personal level.

Since we will soon be talking about each of Mary's sandtrays in detail, I will end this part of the introduction to her case by briefly mentioning the fifth sandtray (Figure 43), since it gave me my first real clue as to how we should work together. I cannot begin to put into words the depth of feeling which this produced in us as we viewed it together. I was quite moved by the "little lost girl" figure, so much so that I asked whether the white polar bear was attacking or protecting it. Mary began to cry. I waited, and then she told me about the deep pain and sense of rejection-which she thought she had forgotten—when she was two or three and had been shut up in a large hospital. Her mother had been forbidden to stay with her during and after she had corrective surgery on her harelip. Incidentally, she said the memory still makes her feel ugly and unattractive. After this session there was no longer any doubt about transference and countertransference—and so our work began in earnest, sometimes with dreams, sometimes with sandplay, and sometimes just talking and sharing.

Mary was born of Jewish parents, and spent her early years in the southern part of the country. Her father was an attorney, and Mary told me that he seemed to care very little, if at all, for his Jewish background and religion. Mary expressed a need in herself for some religious connection; so I suggested she might do some reading and perhaps attend Temple for some services if she felt so inclined. I must say that when she married several years later, it seemed as though both families were happy and relieved that both were Jewish, and enjoyed the fact that the ceremony was celebrated in the traditional manner.

When Mary first came to see me, she expressed a deep feeling of always having been cut off from her mother. She said she experienced her father as a rather stoic person, always working at keeping out any sentiments of negativity in the family. It was definitely understood that father's peace and quiet be protected at all times. As older teenagers, Mary and her brother (two years older than she) both left home, but both were financially somewhat dependent on their parents. Both went on to college and graduate school, partly because of what Mary at least felt was a parental push for deciding on a career right away. Many of Mary's early dreams were of the family home being covered with snow and ice, which points to the lack of communication in the family.

Soon after leaving home in her late teens, Mary started living with a man much older than herself. She described him later as an extension of her own father, very much into his "head" and cut off from feeling—or at least unable to communicate feeling. I will later explore this area of her life in some detail, since her dreams and sand pictures depicted this rather negative relationship—and her struggle to break it off creatively—quite clearly.

Mary is one of the few clients I have been fortunate enough to have kept some contact with over the years; she is now a married professional with a young son. I also know her parents slightly, and it is always good to observe the dramas of families as they unfold. Best of all was to witness the growing and creative relationship between Mary and her partner. During her therapy with me, Mary was still struggling hard and faithfully to achieve a deep and committed relationship with her mother; her father now seems proud of his daughter and grandson, but still can't express much closeness to either of them. This was even more true at the time of therapy.

Mary's inability to express anger towards me as a mother-figure caused some problems, but this was partly due to my own difficulty in this area. It did, however, resolve, which helped make our relationship deeper and more productive during most of the time we were working together (not always weekly).

With so much concentration on matriarchal consciousness, it is not surprising that this area developed quickly. However, as will be noted in descriptions of the individual sand pictures, it should be quite clear that Mary developed her own patriarchal inner and outer qualities as well, and at what seemed a very conscious level. This of course came only after much hard work with the sand and dream images—in a safe and protected space, which includes the safety and protection afforded by the therapist as well.

———

Mary's first sandtray and central theme (Figure 39) is the road, or journey, up through a kind of bridge or labyrinth of driftwood, and passing by a snake-like creature on the way. The boat in the right front of the tray is quite tiny, and it seems to lead to the mountain-like castle-house on the right. The roads are winding and circuitous.

No doubt this image does depict Mary's way or journey at the time—some confusion perhaps, but much movement and struggling. She mentioned the snake as feeling like her own sexuality, and since this was a great concern of hers in her current relationship, it makes this all seem accurate. She said that the bear was important and that the bird-creature was ungainly. She liked the three hills molded in the sand.

I kept thinking about what Mary was telling or experiencing, and why she seemed rather fearful and unsure in spite of her seeming to enjoy the production, which obviously was real to her. It felt to

FIGURE 39

me that the image was just where Mary was — needing and desiring

FIGURE 40

a real journey in life, but knowing that her boat, or maybe her ego at that time, was somewhat fragile, and certainly small. At first I thought the scene somewhat unfriendly, maybe because of the snake's position and the phallic thrust of the sand—right into the small boat, it seemed. However, since she obviously enjoyed making the scene and seemed more at ease when it was finished, I felt better about it as well, and began to pick up what seemed, at first, to have been deeply hidden messages.

Mary's second sandtray (Figure 40) is somewhat strange as well, but makes more sense when viewed more symbolically and at a deeper level. The entire sand picture makes a kind of clown face, which Mary called a "monkey face." Later she said it represented her as the "always-pleaser." The red figure seems to form the nose of the large face, but is really a telephone booth. Later, as we viewed some of her slides, Mary said she felt this telephone was there because communication between her and her male friend was so very bad. The rest of the image makes a kind of elongated circle emphasized by driftwood and animals and three peasant women. A strong white horse placed in the left top corner completes the figure. The energy of this special white horse looking over the entire sandtray feels good.

FIGURE 41

I knew Mary wanted and needed more understanding of her dark archetypal urges and images. I hoped she was capable of taking a risk. I enjoyed the funny clown face, and the circling animals seemed friendly. I too saw the telephone as underscoring her need or lack of personal communication.

Mary said the elephant was awkward and ungrounded, like herself, and it is easy to see this looking at the back right corner of the tray (Figure 41), the two very large rocks it is standing on being neither stable nor firm. The beautiful Monterey pine to the left seems quite rooted, and the bridge down to the water could be the link between conscious and unconscious, as well as a slide or diving board, as she called it. She said the dwarf was quite friendly and that the animals were circling around him. Later she told me the sandtray represented the beautiful side of what she wanted in her life. Fortunately or unfortunately, she had shared a significant dream just beforehand, which I recorded as dream four (later in text).

Obviously, Mary is wise to choose the longer, slower path. All in all, my intuition and feeling wondered why she didn't do more playing in her sand pictures, since this seemed to be just what she needed at the time. Healing can take different paths at different times, and it often works in strange ways.

Two months later, Mary made her first attempt at play (Figure 42), at least to some extent. She centered the circus animals, point-

FIGURE 42

ed towards the rear of the tray, with the dog sitting in the tree at the right center, and the King underneath the tree. The dog opens its mouth and sticks out his tongue when pressed in a certain place. Mary felt this to be a kind of spoof—pleasing on the outside, but revealing anger on the inside. It seemed as though she were playing to humor me. On the left of the tray are several warriors, an Indian warrior among them. There is a large white lamb inside the outdoor cooking triangle, which even afterwards she could not explain. She will later use this lamb several times in her sandtrays, in most cases to express the theme of sacrificing her own feelings. This was especially true at the time of this picture. She said that the lovely peacock, right in the center in front of a lovely tree, represented inner beauty. There is an unfinished house at the rear center, and a peasant woman in the right front corner walking down some rather steep steps.

The peacock can represent the eyes of the gods, and sometimes ego-inflation, but the way it is centered with the living tree just in front hints at the image's potential significance. Mary's anger was somewhat unconscious, but I did feel it, and I understood and appreciated the coming long struggle and pain that I felt her journey would take her on.

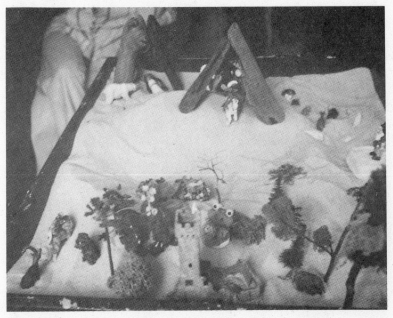

FIGURE 43

It is important to pay particular attention to the beautiful spiraling of the male Indians (Figure 43)—away from the home tent and out into the world of forests and adventure, it seemed. The most moving part was obviously the little girl, either protected or threatened by the white polar bear, and sheltered by driftwood in the shape of a teepee. Mary's rather quiet weeping told me more, as she recounted the harelip-surgery episode mentioned earlier. She said she had not remembered or been aware of the extent of her grief until this day. This of course told me we could now trust each other, and I hoped she could open up more to her life and journey. I too feel that dwarfs are special, so perhaps this one was a potential wonder-worker. The frog may be a fantasy, but I related it to some type of transformation now or in the future.

The next sandtray (Figure 44) was not too surprising after Mary's last one, and it still feels like a very clear picture of transformation of the psyche and/or self. It is a moving time. The placing of the delicate little cherry tree and seahorse (both male and female) in a small pond of water right in the center of the tray makes this quite clear as an image. I feel that both the cars and the animals are circling around the pond, and it is interesting that this time Mary chose a prehistoric or old elephant. She told me later that she had to begin integrating the city and nature in her life. Another contrast is the old witch-mother in the left front corner, directly across from the little girl with whom Mary identified. She said that this little girl was the good girl (herself). The rest of the picture is again made up of earth-spirits, trees, driftwood, and this time a very large turtle. One last but important item was the little Chinese junk which

FIGURE 44

she placed on the vessel-like piece of clay. She told me this represented "the hope of heaven." At the time I was unsure of this, but since she used the same boat several times later, with a similar symbolic meaning, I was able and happy to accept her explanation and to see the sense of it all.

This sandtray brought about in me mostly deep feelings and intuition that Mary's own symbolic self had come to the surface, out of or into the water. I felt a coming together or centering of her outer ego as well. More words are redundant at this point, since the sand picture speaks for itself. I feel I *knew* that healing was taking place, and I was grateful and happy for Mary.

In between Figures 44 and 45, Mary was somewhat overwhelmed with negative dreams about the young man with whom she was involved. A few of these I will briefly discuss in another section; for now it is enough to say that one was of lizards in their bed with them, and her trying not to be afraid. Figure 45 is difficult to understand by just looking at it, but Mary did share one of its main elements: she said that the man's head is being pushed down by the two bridges on either side of it. At the time she told me she was literally trying to push the young man's head down; later she realized that there simply was too much head stuff in the relationship and not enough of the heart. The theme of the Indian ritual appears again, this time very alive and active. Most importantly, the Indians seem to be returning to their tepees — with food, etc. —

FIGURE 45

instead of leaving. Mary placed two totems in this picture, as well as the Monterey pine on the back left part of the tray. The spirals are quite clear, as is all the movement. It seems as though the large owl is overlooking the entire tray, especially the Indians and the few women nearby.

There seems to be a real development for Mary, of her inner masculine in particular. The lovely cavelike center and the beautiful authentic Indian bowl placed carefully in the tree, like a nest, clarifies the feminine. There seems to be more of a coming together of the male and the female, and a growing knowledge that there needs to be more in a real relationship between man and woman than merely the "head," thinking aspect. Mary needed more heart communication. The picture points to definite development, which seems to some extent conscious. I feel the owl perhaps represents Athena (intellect), but with its great wings spread it could also be a protector, an all-seeing helper.

In my experience with sandplay therapy, it always seems to happen (perhaps more with women than with men, but certainly with both) that after a move upwards one must go into the depths of the sea, and maybe to the heights of the moon as well. One must literally dig up or find some contact with the unknowable. It seems clear that gold cannot be founwithout digging deep, or risking confrontation with whatever the unconscious brings into the sandtray.

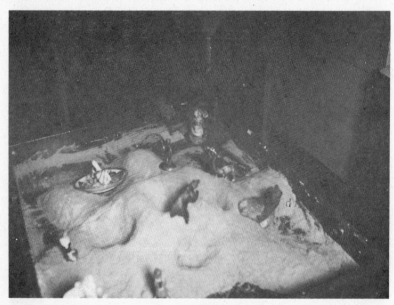

FIGURE 46

Thus Mary dug her holes deep and molded the sand carefully, so that her entire picture (Figure 46) looks like some sort of sea creature. The broom is meant to be a huge tree reaching to the sky, and Mary said she was putting a kind of nature spirit or creature in front of this, with other trees around as well. The animals she chose were a bear riding a log with his eyes covered, and a prehistoric bear placed as though to confront it. There are figures of a boy and a girl (Hansel and Gretel), as well as another young boy fishing for a very large fish. The picture also uses another prehistoric animal, as well as a piece of carved statue.

This kind of sandtray is necessary for in-depth analysis using sandplay; it seems to be mainly a real attempt to make conscious the partly unknowable. In any case I knew Mary was destined to dig deep and reach high on her special journey.

Four months later: Mary said that this sandtray (Figure 47) gave her "a feeling of inner power" (this was a time in which Mary was involved in a new, seemingly quite creative relationship). The image looks like an upper leg or thigh, a fact of which neither she nor I was aware while she was molding the sand. She added more about the picture, saying that she liked the roaring rhino. There

FIGURE 47

is some kind of crossing over the bridge, and an old man is showing the way. The fox or wild dog is eyeing all this, perhaps deciding who will be allowed to cross. The Noah's ark was made in fun;

it is like a myth or a beginning. Other figures she used are, again, two large pieces of driftwood, which this time seem to be embracing each other. The same large Monterey pine reappears. There are several interesting animals in the picture, as well as an umbrella, a red wheel, and a small Buddha behind the foot.

In addition to Mary's comment, I was struck by the small, lovely Buddha near the "foot." Both Buddha and foot are religious symbols. The foot has a deep meaning in Judaism, signifying groundedness, stepping forward, and keeping to the path. I had not, initially, been too aware of how Mary was molding parts of the body in her sand pictures—even in the first there is clearly a face, perhaps monkey or clown-like. From some angles the picture looks like the upper part of a leg; yet from another angle I can see a seahorse, which certainly fits in with Mary's ongoing development. Strange as it seems, when much later (long after Mary and her new friend had returned from a trip to Nepal) we looked again at some of the pictures, Mary suddenly became very excited and said that the shaky

FIGURE 48

bridge brought back some images of that moving trip, especially the actual bridges they had crossed while there. It had been a very deep time for Mary and her friend, a scary and stressful time but also a beautiful and joyful one. The two had experienced profound sharing; they were certain they now wanted to be together permanently.

Mary called Figure 48 "a sacrificial ritual." The lamb is now on the outside, watching. Mary felt that the "head stuff" was now burning in a deep ritual way, and that the four small lizards must be burned as well. The king first seen in Figure 49 is watching. Some animals are playing. She called the tepee a "sacred" place or space. The soldiers seem to be keeping order. The Monterey pine seems more alive this time, activated by several people and animals, even a green snake sitting in the branches watching the process. There are more people near the dark king.

I remember the awe and religious feeling generated by the image—despite the crude earthiness of the tepee, or maybe because of it. When Mary lit a candle inside the androgynous clay figurine (the one with both a male and a female face), it felt as though we were *participating* in the sand picture. There seemed to be some sort of presence in the cave-like temple Mary molded.

FIGURE 49

Three months later: Figure 49 seems like a different kind of spectator scene, with a man looking through his glasses at the women clumsily climbing the hills toward the Greek goddesses. The animals on the left are wild, and thus may need to be made more conscious. At the time, Mary said that the strange, decorated clay piece is like an old comic-book character (The Thing); it is ugly but watchful. In her own words, Mary was "feeling fearful and not quite good enough—sort of separated" (she was in the middle of studying for her psychologist's license exam). Among the more or less demonic animals are the sea-horse and, over to the right, a butterfly. The boat, though still small, is larger than the earlier ones and seems sturdier.

I was struck by the awkwardness of the women climbing up the hill. I noted that the ladders or paths were very shaky and certainly not too grounded. The climb towards individuation is not always easy, and the struggle is sometimes unsure and awkward. Men seem to be forced to keep going and finding stronger ways to climb. This is expected of them, and more recently, of women too.

I like the humor in this sandtray; with all Mary's stress at the time, she seemed able to see the fun of it all. I am not sure if she was aware that the animals on the left side tend to be demonic and fearful-representing, no doubt, some symbolic part of herself that would need to be dealt with, or at least recognized soon. There is a struggle within the picture, which is perhaps why the sea-horse is there as a helper or guide.

FIGURE 50

Mary said that this sandtray (Figure 50) was an attempt to integrate the hills from her last sandtray; and this one does feel more harmonious:

> I am the one traveling in the drawn rickshaw; I am trying hard to move. The duck seems too high up, but the owl seems just right and the birds are great. I like the colors. The witch by the castle is still watching. I know I have to climb to be in better connection with my self-esteem.

There are two bears on the left side of the hill; one has its eyes closed, but seems to be leading the mother-bear. There are many flowers, shrubs, and small ceramic tiles, maybe as paths, but as decoration as well. The large owl is standing on two big rocks, and the wise old man is just in front of the rocks, apparently looking over the whole process.

My first impression of the tray was that it is like a spiraling mountain. As a painter, I always have to be careful not to over-project my own images of the entire sand model, but in viewing this image I immediately saw a lovely floppy-eared dog with seductive eyes right in the center of the picture. I still see this and feel it to be symbolically quite right. Mary's real need at the time might well have been for a sympathetic dogguide. She had actually told me,

FIGURE 51

earlier, about her dog, which had been killed when Mary was a teenager, an event from which she suffered deeply. She shared with me several dreams about this dog, the animal sometimes dead and sometimes joyously playful. The beautiful colored glass and stones, as well as the green trees, are beautiful. In one corner are the two dwarfs or miners, and this time they seem to be meeting. Mary later said that the picture made her feel very good and gave her a warm, peaceful inner feeling. Certainly, the wise old man and the witch seem to have made a positive connection.

One month later: This picture (Figure 51) is of four rounded mounds of sand molded and balanced to fill the sandtray. Each mound is connected to the other by a bridge, clearly a breast-image — not that the mounds could not be hills instead of breasts, at another time or for another person. Given prior associations and the fact that Mary had been unconsciously (and at times, almost consciously) molding parts of her own body in the sand, the interpretation of these mounds as breast-images is justified — it is also my own intuition. The images show a profound development in one side of the feminine, perhaps related to the bonding and nurturing Mary felt she did *not* receive from her own mother.

In one of the sets of connected mounds, Mary placed a seated white cow; she put a small cherry tree right in the middle, with two dwarves emerging from behind. There is a small starfish in front of the mound, as well as some decorative shrubs and butterflies. She put a lone snake quite high on one piece of driftwood. The blue and red magic horses face each other, with a white clay horse in the extreme back, near the dwarves. Lastly, she placed the polar bear inside a toothpick fence, which Mary said was to keep him in; she did not want him to leave. She actually said very little about the picture until much later, though she did say that it was very feminine. To me the sandtray is in fact an honoring of the feminine, portrayed as quite nurturing (the double set of breasts); the white cow in the center seems almost sacred, and certainly connects with the nurturing feminine Mary needed in the outer world. She seems to be aware that the strength of the polar bear is what is now needed in her own life. Knowing how frightened Mary had once been as the little girl lost, it seemed quite positive to see her sheltered by the strength of the bear.

Figure 52 shows a coming together of the masculine and feminine; it is a moving and spiraling picture, with the feminine on the left in the form of a bowl or uterus, and a more active right side, with its phallic thrust directly in and back out of the cave. She used the little fisherboy once again, putting him in the center of the animal life. The seahorse is coming out of the cave and looks like it is following the big swan. Mary said that this was her way of searching for inner beauty. Most of the outer animals seem masculine, but the lovely ram is both that and feminine, having a rounded body and curled horns. The sea-shells Mary used seem to make the picture even more feminine and balanced.

FIGURE 52

My feelings and thoughts about the sand picture involved the spiral of life—masculine and feminine, city and nature—moving in a kind of cosmic harmony. The cave could be a place of retreat, or a feminine uterus or birth canal with a sort of phallic bridge over it. The bowl-shaped center is indeed feminine, with its shells beautifully placed and the animals coming in and out. Mary lived in the city, and part of her struggle was always between "city life" and "natural life." The picture shows an attempt to bring the two closer, in more harmonious contact.

Two months later: Looking at Figure 53 both inwardly and outwardly, it too seems to portray a feminine uterus or birth canal, though the picture as a whole is quite different from the preceding one. First, after shaping the triangular figure surrounded by water, Mary had a large prehistoric elephant coming for water almost into the center of the tray. The same witch-mother is used again, but the king is different. Both the witch and the king seem to be protecting or watching the children and infants near the house and water. The rest of the scene is filled with small ceramic tiles, lovely decorations which children in therapy often call "candy" or "treasure." In the back right corner is a flowering, orange-brown bush, as well as the large piece of driftwood Mary had used on several other occasions.

FIGURE 53

This sand picture is no doubt a continuation of Mary's growing involvement with the feminine in herself. Symbolically and literally it is a beautiful picture, with the lovely stream encircling the inner feminine, and showing the vulnerability of a woman when she fully opens up to life. The little dwarf and the Noah, or shepherd,

FIGURE 54

or protector, are in the right place to quietly oversee all that is happening. Perhaps this shows, once again, the need for a safe and protected shelter. The bridge seems to connect to what Mary calls her fantasy world.

Three months later: Mary described Figure 54 as a kind of death-struggle between her and the person with whom she is involved. Mary seemed to recognize that the three-mound triangle represented breasts, but this time the Indian warriors were fighting right on top of these vulnerable things. There is one Indian in a canoe and another apparently guiding him. There are two trees, under one of which is a large mouse standing up and looking wise; Mary called him "earthy." A man and a woman are kneeling, one towards the large foot mentioned earlier, the other towards a very small foot. Mary later mentioned that it felt as though both figures were honoring spiritual goodness.

At first I was concerned by the seeming violence in the image, but since Mary had been having associated dreams, I was somewhat prepared. I knew she and her friend had to do battle temporarily to bring their feelings out in the open. Struggle is sometimes necessary before reaching a dignified and harmonious place to live; thus sand pictures are healing even if they are a little frightening at first.

More needs to be said about the man and woman kneeling before the respective feet. When Mary said they were honoring spiritual goodness, I thought of the old tradition of foot-washing, especially the story of the women washing the feet of Jesus. One must start out on one's journey with firm feet and a direct relationship with the firmness of the earth. Feet support the body, and they have been called symbols of the soul.

Three months later:

Figure 55 quite clearly shows the head and shoulders of what looks like a female figure. I feel that the peacock and the woman facing each other are not exactly friendly (more work was going on between Mary and her friend, who for several weeks had both been involved in a small group of couples working on relationship problems). In the sandtray there seems to be danger and war in the air. There is a Zulu warrior on the left side of the tray, and warplanes flying around threateningly — directly across from the two children. The large black frog seems to guard the bridge across the water.

Mary apparently still has some unresolved anger, and her head is still too much in command. In actual life, however, things were working out very creatively for Mary, who felt that her friend was beginning to listen and hear her feelings more deeply. Maybe there has to be a crisis before all can be resolved. Mary thought the planes were there partly because she and her friend had just flown to Los Angeles to visit his parents. The women on horses in the center of the picture seem positive and to be bringing in energy, and the two feminine goddesses (winged victory and the little mother of Knossos) reinforce that impression.

FIGURE 55

In Figure 56 many small babies are enjoying the sun and water. Mary felt that they were out of the womb and free, but she also saw that they were in danger, since there seemed to be war waging all around. Mary said, again, that she had put the boat in the drift-wood vessel because it was her fantasy of heaven, and the image was always helpful to her. The waterbearer in the front of the tray is standing firm, perhaps carrying the water of life. The two sand molds with the babies on top remind one of embryos; it could be that the vulnerable babies and unborn offspring need his protection. Mary said that although the Indians seemed to be fighting, she felt that they were protective as well. Creativity is sometimes aborted or not fully developed until the time is right.

Perhaps the babies do need to be freed to enjoy the sun and water, but at the same time they need protection. The little island-like mounds may be places of shelter. The picture thus may represent a period of incubation, especially considering the next picture in the series. This picture certainly shows some growth since the preceding one, five months earlier. Mary and her friend were living together more creatively, making plans for a trip to India.

Only nine months separated Figures 55 and 56, but they represent a move from disintegration to the birth of the Mermaid (Mary herself), and thus wholeness. Such a statement is difficult to prove, but I know I have experienced some marvelous moments of what seem like eternity while working with many of my patients, and Mary was no exception. Sometimes the process simply demands much trust between therapist and patient.

FIGURE 56

Four months later: It seems that Mary has resolved her "city" problems by literally enclosing herself in — or adopting — the figure of a living mermaid. This started out very unconsciously, as always, and the completed picture (Figure 57) was a big surprise to both of us. It does make sense, however, since Mary very much enjoys water and relates well to it both outwardly and inwardly. Her latest therapy work had been related to the world "outside," so the inner mermaid seemed a good balance. Mary and her friend were now seriously planning their marriage. She still wanted to do a few sand-trays and to keep in contact as much as possible. The body shape is obviously the most absorbing element in the picture; it seems real and full of motion.

One month later: Figure 58 is full of what seems like archetypal material and very powerful animals or instincts. Mary felt it focused on her relationship with her fiancé and the fact that she was gathering strength in order to pass all her examinations and get her state counseling license. There is a Balinese dancer in the back left corner, and Mary's foot-symbol is right in the middle, to guide her. The picture is full of large elephants, including the sacred white one. The path across the bridge to consciousness and the outer world seems safe, but Mary knows she must watch out for the alligators-which are in the water where they belong, but are ready to grab at perhaps the wrong time.

FIGURE 57

The sandtray was difficult to understand, for both of us; it seemed so different and unknown. It was obvious that Mary felt energy after making the picture, however, so I took my cue from that, and

FIGURE 58

remembered that even many of the children I had worked with would sometimes have a session and then say "the dead gods are coming to life." Maybe this is what is happening in this picture. Certainly the elephants are strong. There was a small foot (one she had not used before) on the bridge, and two lovely apple trees in full fruit at opposite corners of the sandtray. I accepted this picture as it stood, and did not attempt to rationalize it further.

Figure 59 is the last sand picture Mary made with me, and it seems to integrate much of her inner and outer work and life. She did not talk much about the picture at the time, but said it felt peaceful and related. It looks simple in the slide — a large feather to the side, a mirror reflecting many things, some Indians riding and walking, some shrubbery. There are dwarves, five boats, and a lovely totem pole. There is a little house over by the feather. The shells are pretty, as are the flowers.

FIGURE 59

The image seems quiet and loving compared to the last one, and it seemed to help Mary resolve some of her disturbances in the outer world. The mirror is certainly a reflection of much of her life. (A little girl once told me that of course the mirror was god. She said it so simply and so assuredly that I knew it too; so I never forgot).

Mary seemed to have plenty of choices available to her; not too many people are given five boats for their journey. The dwarves are right in the center to continue helping her. The masculine and feminine seem to have reached a peaceful resolution; the fully-developed apple tree and flowers reappear in the picture.

A little more should be said about the mirror and the fact that it reflects back out to us. It appears by having the mirror do so, and by having the reflection encompass the feather as well, Mary was expressing the fact that she was indeed seeing more meaningful images unfolding and becoming clear. Whether her feather represented air or bird, or was simply an adornment, or was all three, I felt that Mary saw it in the more religious sense of emptiness, lightness and faith. There are Native American myths in which the feather points the way to heaven, and that seems to fit this last picture more accurately. Both this and the preceding picture seem to be related to the progress of Mary's inner journey, as well as to her upcoming outer journey to India and Nepal, and even to her impending marriage as well.

———

During the years Mary worked with me in therapy, she brought in many, many dreams, and since some of them are related to her sandplay work, it seems pertinent to recount at least some of them. I will not always relate whole dreams, but rather present the salient parts. In the case of very short dreams, everything will be told.

Interestingly enough, Mary had several dreams which directly led her to come to me. A few of these she did not share with me until a few months after she started producing sandtray pictures. One of these was:

> A woman was standing with her gun in the forest while I watched from the side. An animal started to charge from far away. My therapist [the one Mary worked with before me] was standing behind her. She lifted her gun and shot the animal (lion-hippo), but it kept charging. She had shot it between the eyes and it stopped charging, but another animal behind the therapist jumped on her back and surprised her.

Just before she started working with me she had another dream, which she explained to me by saying she felt she needed "a different kind of food." The dream was that she was in or near a bus station, and at a Zim's fastfood place with some friends, who wanted her to stay and to have a breakfast of bacon, pancakes and eggs. Though it felt good to be with her friends, in the dream Mary told them that she had an appointment with her therapist (naming me), then left. I found it interesting and strange that she would have such an archetypally American dream just at this time.

Mary related another dream about her earlier therapist (this was, again, well after our own work was well underway):

> The therapist was sitting at a table practicing throwing her knife from far off. She threw it high, but it came back toward me and landed right at the juncture of my thumb and first finger. I was nicked and I felt something inside when the blood started flowing heavily, but no pain. I held my hand—she tried to find out if I was all right, and verbally I insist I am.

Mary related the dream to the fact that she felt she had to please everyone, even when hurting herself.

Another interesting dream took place about the time she made the beautiful mandala picture with the (pink) elephant tottering on the two high rocks, trying to decide whether or not to dive or slide into the water (see Figure 41). The dream had Mary on a high balcony, looking at a book by Jung. She thought of jumping off the balcony as that would be a quicker way down to the ground floor. However, she decided instead to take the stairs down, as the other way was too steep and dangerous.

Mary felt this dream helped bring her closer to earth, even if she herself did feel awkward and somewhat unconnected. In Hindu mythology there are lovely myths and stories about the elephant once being a part of the clouds and the Milky Way. At one point they disturbed a gifted teacher [sage?] on earth; as punishment they were sent to earth to carry heavy burdens, but they were allowed to carry kings as well. Some myths say elephants are occasionally reunited with clouds, and send us rain. Given the same sandtray picture (Figure 41), another important feature of elephants is that they are socially-inclined and care for their wounded and their young offspring. The parents live apart for some time while mating and birthing, but eventually they return to the herd.

Mary had many shadow and/or negative dreams during her early work with me, most or all of them involving the man with whom she was living. In one of these, she and the man were just sitting together blowing breath into each other's face, and nothing happened. In another, as related in Mary's words:

> I am in bed with my friend and there are lizards there. I try not to be afraid. One of the lizards turns into a mutant girl who is not afraid; she picks up a robin, which pecks her and draws blood. She doesn't care, she's trying to be a friend.

In another dream, her friend says that he is possessed by anima; she asks.him who this anima is, and he tells her, "you." On one occasion she wakes up screeching these words: "If you do not take more responsibility, I'll leave you." He looks very surprised.

In the last dream on this theme, she and her friend were in an institutional setting; they were camping, and a cat jumped on his head, claws extended, although it loved him. Then the cat and mouse were playing at her feet; they began to fight, and the cat yowled and lunged for Mary's throat. Somehow, during the dream Mary was thinking that "...the world is at a dying point—it can't produce its own food."

This dream series occurred within a space of about four months, after the sand picture in which Mary literally pushed a representation of the man's head down into the earth—which she was conscious enough to realize meant that the relationship was definitely too much "in the head." Soon afterwards she was able to leave that relationship with ease and dignity—or perhaps better stated, with heart and creativity.

It seems right to relate one or two dreams which helped Mary understand the apparent coldness she felt in her family, especially from her mother, and the pain she had suffered in the traumatic childhood episode at the hospital, when she had been so isolated from her parents. From her sessions, Mary was increasingly able to realize that her mother had to spend so much time keeping peace and quiet for her Mary's father that the children rarely felt comfortable about or capable of expressing their negative feelings honestly.

The first dream came at the time of Figure 43, which depicts a "little girl lost" and the polar bear which is protecting her:

> I am at the hospital, waiting to be transferred to another hospital for an operation. A nice black man sits in my room eating his lunch; I eat an apple and a banana. The doctor comes and walks with me. He meets his daughter and I watch them kiss on the lips. I feel jealous. I get upset and shed tears—I feel ugly and unattractive. We are now on the street and I see my mother hurriedly trying to cross it, but she is crying. I run up to her after a while, when I see that she will not come to me. Finally, I call her name and then hug her. We are both crying; she obviously was not coming to the hospital. I go on with the doctor.

Other dreams on this theme centered around her parents' house being surrounded by snow. In one, a monster tree suddenly came to life; Mary tells her parents that it will be okay, and she rushes to her mom to get the weapons that scientists had left them—a blue needle dart pen:

> I shoot and the tree is rooted to its spot, but it seems like it will come back to life again. Mom said to fire four more shots. There is more in this dream, about rats and cats in the living room and mom trying to chase them out.

There was another rather long dream about Mary's mother being pregnant and ready to give birth:

> I can see the body lying sideways in her stomach. I touch it, my eyes closed. There's a little boy in the room who seems to be a spirit of the baby. I want to talk with him, but mom is bitchy and angry towards me. When I talk she tells me not to poison his mind with things he'll remember later. For me it's like talking to a brother. He is very wise. Mom gets so uptight that we leave and go into the den. I crack nuts and listen to the information from *him*.

As she developed in her analysis and sandtray work, Mary had a few more positive dreams of her mother. She seemed to break some of the archetypal patterns a bit more quickly after she found herself able to express anger towards me; she found it not so terrible to show some anger more creatively. She had many dreams about her father as well, but I will present only one, since it best seems to express her early feelings, in addition to perhaps shedding light as to why her first relationship was so negative:

> There is some kind of big fly with huge wings in my parents' house. I hit it, but it just becomes bigger and bigger, then it changes into a dog which runs around the house. I am very scared but no one in the family does anything. Another man chased it outside; the animal turned into a skunk, sprayed, then ran away. This older man walked inside and said he had killed the animal with a kitchen knife. My father was right there all the time, but he never turned into a man of action. I hugged the other man, and felt like I had been rescued by a story-book white knight.

The last dream series has to do with Mary's relationship to the man she later married. He was a college teacher a bit older than herself, not as developed as her on the emotional side, though eager to change and "be more human," as he put it. In one dream, they are in a building together, and the building is slowly sinking. Mary gets out and runs away. The scene was a flood, and in the dream Mary knew she could swim. In another dream the two were surrounded by snow. Mary told me that she was really affected by these dreams—she and her friend had decided not to live together for a short period, and according to Mary, "I was feeling that he wasn't bound to me, or that we weren't grounded."

Later, after they were together, Mary dreamed that they were standing outside, in the presence of four animals:

> One is an elephant. Darts are being shot at me, and I hold my arms up to protect myself. An armored, armadillo-like rhinoceros animal is next to me. I pet it and tell my friend he shouldn't be scared of it—it won't harm us. I can see its stubby eyes sticking out from underneath the armored body

In the last dream, Mary is with her friend; she is pregnant.

> I discover that it's very close to the time (nine months). I am in the doctor's office and I am scared—of course I will keep the baby, even though I am very young. I'm scared because I haven't learned any breathing techniques. I have to give a name—at first I say *Smith* [Mary's maiden name]—then I say my friend's last name; he's the father. At some point I feel the water break, and it's okay.

I should mention one dream involving Mary's mother, in which Mary, her mother, and I are visiting a well-known Jungian analyst at his home. We talk about dreams, and Mary's mother is impressed. She says that older Jungian men are funnier and softer. Later, Mary dreamed about receiving a green frog: "It has an open mouth and I look at it a lot." Two nights later Mary dreamed of her mother's death, and how in the dream it took several days for her to fully feel and react.

The last three dreams just as clearly relate to Mary's changing attitude towards her personal mother. The green frog seems to be a harbinger of transformation, and I understand the mother's dream-death as being the "death" of Mary's own inner negative mother.

Mary was twenty-three years old when she first came to see me, not married but living with a man about ten years her senior. She was enrolled in a psychology program in an area university, and had taken some classes in Jungian psychology. She was "seeking" but did not know which path to take. Her main problems as she expressed them were: uncertainty and confusion about her relationship, her poor physical self-image (even though she was and is quite attractive), and her deep feeling of being cut off from her mother, with little connection to her father, either. Most of all, she sought some kind of religious connection. She felt that her parents denied any kind of religious faith, having themselves long ago abandoned their own Jewish background.

Mary loved dance and swimming and felt quite competent doing both. She had trouble expressing her own feelings of inadequacy and inner anger, and "covered up" by presenting a kind of proud, quiet, almost arrogant demeanor and behavior. The other side of this persona, however, was her need to continually please everyone around her, especially her therapist at the time. Since it was difficult for her to express her real feelings, at least at first, it took time — and especially much sandtray work — to "get at" what she was truly capable of in her life.

Mary came to me with many defenses. She had given me the impression that she was in a graduate program, and about ready for her counseling license, and therefore wanted to learn about sandplay for her own practice. Since I knew about the fascination sandplay exerts on many people, I was willing to listen and let her experience sand pictures for herself — at least to make a few pictures. I am glad I did so, because it worked out that her psyche did lead her far, and very shortly she realized that what she really wanted and needed was her own reconnection through analysis, deep dream work, and sand pictures.

I like the way Estelle Weinrib explains the developmental process in sandplay therapy. Dora Kalff's and Erich Neumann's developmental stages in children are basically the same, and are certainly valid in terms of what I have experienced with patients, both children and adults — though with adults I view the process a bit more inwardly. As clearly as I can, I will now express what I felt happened with Mary, and how this echoes a more general developmental process in work with most adults and some children. I want to add that I have worked with many adults, both men and women, and never has any individual path followed exactly that of any other — which is why I considered sandplay such a wonderful way to work with people in therapy.

Mary's initial sandtray (Figure 39), though somewhat confused, was a realistic picture of where she was in life — on a journey and in perhaps too small a boat, afraid of powerful and probably undifferentiated sexuality, and willing to drift back into the relative safety of fantasy. Figure 40 has more or less the same themes, but with some attempt at centering, and a recognition of her continuing need to please and to communicate better with others, especially her male friend (at this point I did not feel Mary was fully conscious of all this, though she became more so as we worked through the material).

Figures 41,42, 43, and again more deeply in Figure 46, clearly show Mary's early desire and later ability to descend very low and to explore the heights through work with the personal shadow—in other words, to find the gold, the healing potential and the trust to follow her inner figures.

I feel that Figure 44 quite clearly shows the emergence of the Self in Mary. I also feel the power of the spiraling back-and-forth, and later, of the centering. Some differentiation of the opposites is apparent in this picture, but more clearly in Figures 47 and 50 , and very clearly in Figures 57 and 59.

Mary's new and vulnerable ego went through many struggles, especially in differentiating between her masculine and feminine aspects. I feel that much of this was accomplished by the earlier work on matriarchal consciousness. I also feel that the patriarchal level of consciousness came later, but also through her work and struggle in her earlier pictures and in the outer world as well. Part of this later struggle seemed in some ways lonely, since I for the most part could just be there, though as an important part of the "sheltered space" where this newness could be born and developed.

It became apparent that Mary's spiritual and/or transpersonal aspect had to be born, maybe even several times over. First, the Indians began their rituals in Figures 43, 45 and possibly even Figure 47 as well. Figure 48 shows this, but it is more clear in Figures 52, 54 and Figure 56. Yet Mary's deep acceptance of a need for change, as expressed in Figure 57, seems to have gradually led to her last picture. It is clear that Mary experienced real movement and growth from the matriarchal to the patriarchal level of consciousness, as her later pictures show.

The path towards individuation is never easy, for either woman or men. It was good to observe Mary's unique way of accepting as necessary her life in the city, the full-bodied inner mermaid, and the way of the Native American—the feather to guide and the mirror to reflect. Part of the acceptance always seems to be that the journey is endless but worth the struggle. I feel sure that Mary had conscious knowledge of this at the end of her work with me; and I know that she continues to grow and create, and to face struggles bravely and more consciously.

12

TWO SYMBOLS
The Owl and the Bear

Two animals—the owl and the bear—appear so frequently in children's sand pictures that I have become especially interested in them. I feel that the bear and the owl must evoke some commonality of inner and outer wisdom that needs to be more fully understood. These two such seemingly different animals apparently have deep symbolic significance in the human psyche.

Indeed, in myths and fairy tales the bear symbolizes instinctual wisdom; the owl, spiritual knowledge. But the symbolism of both is ambivalent, that is, both have positive and negative value. Although fierce when defending her young, the bear can be friendly to humans at other times. The bear is also represented in many legends and myths. In Greek mythology, the bear is associated with Artemis, goddess of the hunt. In the Gilgamesh epic, which is certainly the Persian equivalent to Genesis in terms of its basic nature and universal importance, animals often play musical instruments, but only bears dance. It seems that bears have always been identified with the playful, instinctual side of human nature. Perhaps children and adults who use the sandtray know that to get in touch with their own instincts they must get in touch with the bear and invite it to dance once more.

In my research, I have read some very moving North American Indian stories. They show that many tribes greatly respected the bear. Although they ate the bear for food, they also worshipped him in their religious rituals and honored him as a friend to man. Their stories tell of wearing the bear's fur in order to remain friends with him. Many Indian tribes have stories of human mothers who suck-

le bear cubs in great pain, showing a very close and loving identification with the bear.

An old Finnish tale tells quite clearly of the respect and love for
the bear prominent in many early cultures. A verse from "The
Kalevala" says:

> Otso, you're my well-beloved honey-eater of the woodlands,
> Let not anger swell thy bosom.
> I have not the force to slay thee.
> Willingly the life you givest as a sacrifice to Northland.
> Thou hast from the tree descended, glided from the Aspen
> branches—
> Leave thy cold and cheerless dwelling. Come among the
> haunts of heroes,
> Join thy friends in Kalevala. We will never treat thee evil.
> Thou shalt dwell in peace and plenty. Thou shalt feed on
> milk and honey.

In very early bear cults, the head of a slain bear was preserved
and prayed to for several days. The bear was sacrificed in a ritualistic manner. Its blood was not allowed to touch the ground and was
drunk by the men of the tribe. After the sacrifice, the bear meat
was boiled and eaten by every person present, including the young
children. This sort of ritual certainly has much in common with our
modern communion, the symbolic partaking of the blood and body
of Christ. Bear skulls have recently been found in St. Gallen, Switzerland, indicating that bear cults existed there. Remnants of similar cults have been identified in Japan, China, Lapland, Bavaria,
Austria, Yugoslavia and in parts of Western Europe. Bear worship
is also a part of early Eskimo culture. It seems not at all surprising,
then, that the bear has meaning for nearly every culture.

Before I began working with the sandtray, the full significance
of the bear as a living symbol was not clear to me, but I was sure
it was a symbol connected with mother images. One of the first
miniatures I bought was a mother bear who has since had much
of her fur rubbed off by a great deal of loving. But her warm feeling and bright eyes still create a living image for those who find
her on my shelves and rub her back to life.

I now have many bear miniatures in my collection. Some are fierce
bears standing on their hind legs. I have some playful cubs and some
polar bears. The mother brown bear and her two cubs are by far
the most frequently used. One boy used the mother bear and her
cubs in nearly every sand picture he made. Although highly intelligent, he was cut off from his own emotions. Somehow, by using

this bear miniature, he was able to identify with his own instincts, which, in turn, accelerated the healing process. In one striking sand picture (Figure 60), he placed the mother bear in the center of a mandala-like circle. He then placed about fifteen other animals outside and around the circle, saying the mother bear was "teaching" the other animals.

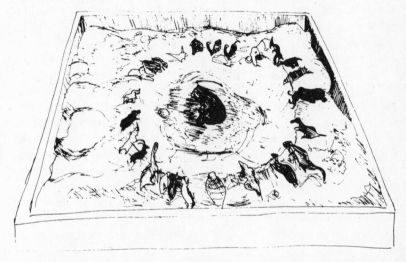

FIGURE 60

I vividly remember one scene by a fourteen-year-old boy when I think about the bear symbol. He, too, was very creative but he was not doing particularly well in school and felt much pressure from his mother and teachers to do better work. In one sand scene, he created a big battle. The last thing he did was place a small house in one corner of the sandtray, with a very large mother bear on the roof. I knew that he was being deluged by negative feedback from both his mother and his teachers at this time. By placing a big bear on a tiny house, he seemed to be expressing the negative weight of the authoritarian females in his life. Eventually, he was able to understand and transform this crushing attention he was receiving from adults into warmer and more mutual relationships.

I also remember one young girl who benefited from her identification with the bear miniature. She had trouble relating to both her parents and was also not doing well in school. Both parents were disappointed in her performance. Her mother in particular stressed doing well in school. After many lovely pictures depicting the mother bear and her cubs in the forest, in caves and protected places, the young girl was able to communicate her feelings to both herself and her parents. She was able to prove that there are meaningful and basic ways of gaining knowledge besides earning good grades. And in the process she gained a great deal of self-confidence.

After this experience of the teaching bear, I decided to examine other children's slides to see how they had used the bear symbol in their scenes. Suddenly I was aware how often others had used the bear, and how it came alive in similar but individually meaningful ways for each child.

If I ask a child, "What does this animal mean to you?," she or he is apt to reply, "But you know, that animal understands me. I can talk to them better than to humans." What they say about the bear or owl may not be as important as how they use these miniatures to tell their own individual stories. After studying these slides in depth, I have begun to develop a feeling for further symbolism of the bear. It is a lunar animal, associated with the moon and the night, yet it is a warm, loving mother by day. The bear then stands for a primitive and perilous part of the unconscious which needs healing; yet it is a symbol of bravery, endurance and strength. Clumsy, gruff and ferocious on the one hand, she is also an animal of wisdom, representing the positive side of mother love. Legend states that she literally "licks" her tiny cubs into shape as soon as they are born.

The real nature of the bear contributes to this symbolism. The females are indeed superior mothers, taking loving and careful care of their young cubs until they are two years old. At that age, the mother bear leaves them alone in a tree, seemingly realizing that she had done all she can for them and trusting they will now learn to survive on their own. She knows they must learn by direct experience and be responsible for their own actions. It is this desire to learn by direct experience that human beings identify with, as well as with the bear's natural wisdom.

Lately adults seem to need this symbol the most; I often see them using the bear in their sand pictures. There seems to be some reason for this. Perhaps the climate of the modern age makes people need to identify with their instincts and recognize the importance of instinctive, nonverbal forms of knowledge. The modern world, with its fast pace and tendency towards assimilations, does not provide us with the time or the opportunity to come into touch with our senses and instinctual roots. Symbolically, the bears themselves seem to be retreating from civilization. So perhaps we humans are internalizing this powerful and needed instinctual symbol. The sandtray provides both children and adults an opportunity to be, to experience, and to know.

I began adding owl miniatures to my collection about five years ago. A four-year-old boy who had been having frequent "monster" nightmares was one of the first to use the very large owl. He called it his "bird monster" and told me he wished to tell the owl not to frighten him so much. I suggested contacting the monster by way of his miniature magic telephone, a toy that he always placed near each of his sand pictures. Bewildered for a moment, he then replied, "I will call the lady with the curly house, [the therapist] so she will talk to him." We carried on a three-way conversation for some time. Somehow this dialogue stopped the boy's monster nightmares almost immediately. It seemed to me the owl did carry its own wisdom.

I started to pay more attention to how other children used owls. Sarah, for example, used them over and over again in her sand scenes. To her, the owl was nocturnal and wise; I am sure she identified with the eerie connotations of the nighttime owl.

Another boy also related very well to the owl symbol. He drew and painted an owl frequently, saying the owl "taught" him. I believed him, for he had certainly learned much about spirituality and the wisdom of the night. He too sometimes irritated his parents and teachers by not getting assignments in on time. But he had an inner wisdom and insight that went far beyond his school assignments.

All the children I have worked with seemed to have had an instinctual awareness that the owl is both wise and scary. As a creature of the night, his enormous eyes frighten children. Nonetheless, they seem to know that owls offer a kind of protection and insight needed in life. They know that the frightening owl can also be an intelligent friend, a friend to light up the path for them at night.

The nocturnal nature of the owl is what identifies it with terror and fear of abandonment and isolation. Although owls are not dangerous, people fear them. In myth, the owl has more often been portrayed as a stranger rather than as a friend to man. Fear of the owl is probably fear of the night and of all the unknown elements which are associated with darkness. The owl's large, glowing eyes which "see all," even in the night, are certainly part of its fearful image.

The Peruvian version of the creation myth casts the owl, rather than the snake, as the tempter which lures a more tragically doomed Eve to a lurid death; while in a Grimm fairy tale entitled "The Owl," an owl is roosting in an abandoned barn and frightens the farmer and all the townspeople. They are so scared they burn down the entire barn to destroy the owl; they are too terrified to deal with the situation in any other way.

The owl has been associated with death and darkness, being often considered the omen of death. It is identified with Satan, the prince of darkness, and with Lilith, goddess of the underworld and harbinger of death. The owl supposedly tricks other birds, causing them to fall into the snares set by hunters. Satan tricks and ensnares humans in a similar manner in religious mythology.

But the other side of the owl's nighttime presence has to do with the poetry and spiritual beauty of the night. A painting by the Russian artist Sulamith Wulfing epitomizes this side of the owl's nature. It shows an owl hovering with its wings extended over a little girl in her night clothes. Other small creatures of the night are huddled around the little girl under the protective canopy of the owl's wings.

Myths express this positive side of the owl's nature. For example, it is identified with Athena, the Greek goddess of wisdom and protectress of heroes. Athena also represents the strong and wise mother. A connection is often made, too, between the resurrection of Christ, giving light in the darkness, and the owl with its eyes like lanterns in the dark forest.

In other legends and fairy tales, the owl is consistently identified with a spiritual, unearthly kind of wisdom, and many children express the same feeling. They often tell me the owl is a kind of protector. Several have said they knew that if the owl were killed, it would bring bad luck. It seems children have some identification with a supernatural quality in the owl. Recently an adult woman placed an owl in her sand picture, but did not understand why. Soon after, she had several dreams in which the owl played an important role. These dreams and the sand picture helped her realize she needed the kind of wisdom the owl represents to improve some of her relationships with other people.

Beyond ancient legends and myths, both the bear and the owl seem to have become part of the fairy tale mythos of the modern world. Gift shops are filled with owl matchbooks, wall plaques, night lights and beer mugs. For children, the bear is a most popular animal. Most children own, or want to own, a stuffed bear to love and cuddle. *Winnie the Pooh, Goldilocks and The Three Bears* and other similar tales exemplify the widespread identification with the bear on the part of children and adults today. Circus artists dress bears in human clothing, suggesting a need to change skins with the bear, to really unite bear nature with human nature, as some Indian tribes actually did in their rituals long ago.

Some children can make a very complete identification with their own instincts. They still know how to dance with the bear and to ask for the protection and wisdom of the owl. They know how to explore their own psyches to find deep connections with the general psychic life of all living things. Perhaps some adults are now able to use their eyes and ears more effectively to make these deep connections as well. Perhaps by listening to the hoot of the owl and the growl of the bear with free and open minds, adults too will learn how to just be or experience, as well as how to know by using their intellects.

I feel the bear and the owl are two moving symbols that help reunite opposites and initiate healing. For the children and the adults who have used these miniatures in the sandtray, the animals have expressed some or all of their multiple and contradictory symbolic meanings. Although the specific meaning each person assigns the miniature is important, the healing process aided by the miniature is far more significant. In the thousands of slides made by both children and adults, it is obvious that both the bear and the owl miniatures are used at very critical times, at times of real importance in treatment.

Who knows how these symbols help in the healing process? One thing is clear and true: when play is creative, it is renewing both the inner and outer life of the individual. The bear and owl are two important symbols because they stir up the fantasy life of the psyche and aid in the everreuniting and healing process.

> Dance, dance, won't you dance with me?
> I am clumsy and gruff,
> But I bring you blessings too.
> The young princess lost her way, but found her Love.
> Where is my mother now?
> She nursed me in pain after she changed her skin for fur.
> They killed my father, but saved his bones; so I could return in my own skin.
> The bears are retreating from the mass of humans.
> But I return to you once more.
> So Humans, can't you dance with me?

TEN YEARS LATER

March 16, 1982

Written by a young man, age seventeen, looking back on his work with me in the sandtray, from ages seven to ten.

During the time that I was involved in sandplay, I may not have understood the effect it had on me, but as I look back on that time now, I gain insight into my early life. I was a child of divorce, before divorce was so common, and I had few peers to relate my problems to. Having someone to talk to, who knew how I felt and what I was going through, helped if not to resolve probelms, at least to voice them.

I see the sandplay as having facilited the communication between myself and Evalyn. As a naturally creative person, I enjoyed building and experimenting with the sand, creating miniature diaramas, and simply talking. I think that in the process of working with my own hands and being occupied with the sandtray, I let some of my guard down. This eased communication, whether or not I was aware of it at the time.

Looking back on the spectrum of my sandplay, I see reflections of a small boy's emotional life. I believe that inadvertently I expressed whatever emotions I felt during the sandtray sessions. I remember that I was asked what some things in my sand pictures represented to me, and this helped me communicate feelings that might not have come out otherwise. The sandtray unconcsiously revealed my feelings. To this day, I continue to express my deepest feelings in art.

BIBLIOGRAPHY

Adler, G. *The Living Symbol*. Princeton: Princeton University Press, 1961.

Aite, Paolo. Communication Through Imagination—Annual of Italian Psychologists, 1977. In *Rivista di Psicologia Analitica*, 1976, and *Journal of Analytical Psychology*, 1978.

Andersen, Hans. *Fairy Tales*. New York: Grosset and Dunlap Publishers, 1945.

Axline, Virginia. *Play Therapy*. New York: Ballantine Books, Inc., 1974.

Bonds, M. *The Bears*. New York: Puffin Books, 1973.

Bradway, Kathryn. Professional Reports, Sixth Annual Conference of Society of Jungian Analysts of Northern and Southern California, San Fransisco, 1979 and *Art Psychotherapy*, 1979.

Campbell, Joseph. *Myths to Live By*. New York: Viking Press, 1972.

————. *The Masks of God—Primitive Mythology*. New York: Viking Press, 1972.

Cirlot, J. E. *A Dictionary of Symbols*. New York: Philosophical Library, 1962.

Cramer, Phebe and Katherine A. Hogan. Sex Differences in Verbal and Play Fantasy. *Developmental Psychology*, 1975.

Craven, M. *I Heard the Owl Call My Name*. Garden City, New York: Doubleday and Co., Inc., 1973.

de Castillejo, Irene. *Knowing Woman—a Female Psychology*. New York: Harper and Row, 1974.

Eickhoff, Louise F.W. Dreams in the Sand. *British Journal of Psychiatry*, 1952.

Erikson, Erik H. Sex Differences in the Play Configurations of Pre-Adolescents. *American Journal of Orthopsychiatry*,1951.

————. *Childhood and Society*. New York: W. W. Norton and Company, 1963

————. *Daedalus, The Woman in America*. Boston: American Academy of Arts and Sciences, 1964.

Fordham, M. *Children as Individuals*. New York: G. P. Putnam, 1969.

Frazer, G. *The Golden Bough*. New York: MacMillan, 1925.

Furth, Gregg.*The Secret World of Drawings*. Boston: Sigo Press, 1988.

Garai, J.*The Book of Symbols*. New York: Simon and Schuster, 1973.

Giedion, S. *The Eternal Present: The Beginnings of Art*. Princeton: Princeton University Press, Bolligen Series XXXV, 1957.

Green, H. *I Never Promised You a Rose Garden*. New York: Signet Books, 1965.

Grimm *Complete Fairy Tales*. New York: Random House Inc., 1972.

Harrison, J. E. *Themis, A Study of the Social Origins of Greek Religions*. Cambridge: Cambridge University Press, 1927.

Henderson, J. *Thresholds of Initiation*. Middletown, Connecticut: Wesleyan University Press, 1967.

Homberger, Erik. *Explorations of Personality*. New York: Oxford University Press, 1938.

Huizinga, J. *Homo Ludens—A Study of the Play Element in Culture*. Boston: Beacon Press,1950.

Jung, C. G. *Man and His Symbols*. New York: Doubleday, 1964.

————. "Mandala Symbolism." In *Collected Works*, Vol. XII. Princeton: Princeton University Press, Bollingen Series XX, 1968.

————. "Psychology and Alchemy." In *Collected Work*, Vol. XII. Princeton: Princeton University Press, Bollingen Series XX, 1971.

Kalff, Dora M. *Sandplay, A Psychotherapeutic Approach to the Psyche*. Boston: Sigo Press, 1981.

Kellogg, R. *Children's Art*. Palo Alto: National Press Books, 1969.

Longfellow, H.W.*The Song of Hiawatha*. New York: Duell Sloan and Pearce, 1891.

Lonnrot, E. *The Kalevala*. Cambridge: Harvard University Press, 1965.

Lowenfeld, Margeret. *The World Technique*. London: George Allen and Unwin, 1979.

Marriott, A. and Sachlin C. *American Indian Mythology*. New York: Thomas Y. Crowell Co., 1968.

Moustakes, Clark E. *Children in Play Therapy*. New York: Ballantine Books, 1973.

Mucehielhi, Roger. *Le Jeau du Monde et le test du Village Imaginaire*, 1960.

Munro, N. G. *Ainu Creed and Cult*. New York: Columbia University Press, 1963.

Neidhardt, John G. *Black Elk Speaks*. Lincoln: University of Nebraska Press, 1961.

Neumann, E. *The Child*. New York: G. P. Putnam & Sons, 1973.

Perry, R. *The World of Animals*. New York: Arco Publishing Co., Inc., 1970.

Reed, Jeannette. *Sand Magic*. Albuquerque, New Mexico: JPR, Publishers, 1975.

Rossi, E. L. *Dreams and Growth and Personality*. Oxford, England: Pergamon Press, 1972.

Stein, R. M. *Incest and Human Love, The Betrayal of the Soul in Psychotherapy*. Dallas: Spring Publications, 1984.

Stewart, Louis. *Sandplay Therapy*. New York: Aesculapius Publishers, 1977.

Storm, H. *Seven Arrows*. New York: Ballantine Books, 1972.

Sullwold, Edith, and Eagle Eye. *The Well-Tended Tree*. New York: Putnam's Sons, 1971.

von Franz, M. L. "Dream and Vision of St. Nilous von der Flue"; "Symbols of the Bear." Unpublished lecture notes, Zadiurich, 1957.

Wells, Herbert George. *Floor Games*. New York: Arno Press, 1975.

Wherry, J. N. *Indian Mask and Myths of the West*. New York: Bonanza Books, 1969.

Wickes, F. G. *The Inner World of Childhood*. Boston: Sigo Press, 1989.

Weinrib, Estelle. *Images of the Self: The Sandplay Therapy Process*. Boston: Sigo Press, 1983.

Zimmer, H. *Myths and Symbols in Indian Art and Civilization*. New York: Harper and Row, 1962.